THE MENTAL GROWTH OF CHILDREN FROM TWO TO FOURTEEN YEARS

UNIVERSITY OF MINNESOTA
THE INSTITUTE OF CHILD WELFARE
MONOGRAPH SERIES NO. XX

D0081764

Success with the block-building test, Minnesota Preschool Scales

10,00

THE MENTAL GROWTH OF CHILDREN FROM TWO TO FOURTEEN YEARS

A Study of the Predictive Value of the Minnesota Preschool Scales

BY

FLORENCE L. GOODENOUGH

PROFESSOR OF RESEARCH
INSTITUTE OF CHILD WELFARE

AND

KATHARINE M. MAURER

INSTRUCTOR IN RESEARCH
INSTITUTE OF CHILD WELFARE
UNIVERSITY OF MINNESOTA

GREENWOOD PRESS, PUBLISHERS
WESTPORT, CONNECTICUT

Library of Congress Cataloging in Publication Data

Goodenough, Florence Laura, 1886-
  The mental growth of children from two to
fourteen years.

  Reprint of the ed. published by the University of
Minnesota, Minneapolis, which was issued as no. 20
of University of Minnesota, Institute of Child Wel-
fare, Monograph series.
  Bibliography: p.
  1. Mental tests. 2. Child study. I. Maurer,
Katharine Mather, joint author. II. Title.
III. Series: Minnesota. University. Institute
of Child Development and Welfare. Monograph series ;
no. 20. [DNLM: BF431 G648me 1942a]
LB1131.G542 1975   155.4'13   70-141548
ISBN 0-8371-5895-8

Originally published in 1942 by the University of Minnesota Press,
Minneapolis

Reprinted with the permission of the University of Minnesota Press

Reprinted by Greenwood Press,
a division of Williamhouse-Regency Inc.

First Greenwood Reprinting 1975
Second Greenwood Reprinting 1976

Library of Congress Catalog Card Number 70-141548

ISBN 0-8371-5895-8

Printed in the United States of America

FOREWORD

In recent years many data have been accumulated from repeated tests of the same children over a substantial period of time. The results of these longitudinal studies have modified many of the concepts that grew out of the earlier cross-sectional studies of children. In particular, the recent controversy on the relative effects of heredity and environment on intelligence test scores has called attention to many new problems that can only be solved by long-time investigations.

In this monograph the detailed results of a longitudinal study are presented in a way that should contribute materially to the forward progress of the techniques of measuring the abilities of young children. A description of the origin and standardization of the Minnesota Preschool Scales, widely used for the study of young children, is followed by a study of the prediction, from measurements made during the preschool period, of later performances on the two revisions of the Stanford-Binet, on the Arthur Performance Scale, and on the Minnesota college ability tests. A discussion of individual cases, with illustrative figures, reveals the manner of growth during childhood.

As is so frequently the case in an extensive study, new scientific problems are raised. One of the most interesting of these arises out of the absence of a relationship of the interval between tests to constancy. This suggests that changes in test content at early levels may be more significant in determining inconsistency of results than are changes in children. There appears also some evidence of sex differences in the rate at which the intelligence quotient stabilizes itself, as well as an unanticipated superiority of the nonverbal scales over the verbal scales at the early ages.

At all age levels the tests are shown to have some predictive value, which persists even up to the age of college entrance. This result appears in spite of the fact that the cases on the uppermost levels used in this study consist of a highly selected group who do not cover the complete range because they entered college early. Not only general ability but special talent seem to be apparent in measurable degree before the children enter school, and both show some tendency to persist up to college entrance. It is clearly indicated that our

v

present tests are not as satisfactory as they might be and that more adequate measuring instruments for both general capacity and special talents are badly needed.

The graphic presentations of individual patterns of growth and the discussion of the cases they represent demonstrate that a single and isolated test of a child, if taken at face value, may lead to serious errors of judgment in working out practical recommendations. The value of several tests, administered at various intervals of time, in determining the child's status and potentiality is clearly shown.

In this monograph the authors suggest a further analysis of the data, to appear later, that will involve the selection of test items at early age levels in terms of their correlation with final status. Enough comment is made on this problem to show how, through the accumulation of longitudinal data and the application of new criteria to the selection of test items, we can, by rebuilding our measuring instruments, make them more effective as practical measures and more meaningful as scientific instruments for determining the child's capacities and attainment. The careful student and the professional worker in the field of mental measurement will find much of value in this monograph.

John E. Anderson
Director, Institute of Child Welfare
University of Minnesota

PREFACE

This is a study of the mental growth of a group of children from the beginning of the nursery school period up to the time of college entrance. Not all children were followed for the entire period. Some moved away from the city. Some parents lost interest in the study and were unwilling to bring their children for further tests. Some dropped out for other reasons. From time to time others were added to take the places of those lost. Thus the personnel of the group has undergone many changes in the course of the twelve-year period. Continuity of a sort has been maintained, however, through the overlapping of the groups from year to year, and a fairly large nucleus has been held constant throughout.

Although we recognize that the resultant data are far from optimal for a longitudinal investigation, it may be noted that the difficulty is common to most long-time studies of this kind. Elimination of a certain portion of the group, as well as the occasional omission of scheduled tests on the part of some individuals, is almost bound to occur whenever an investigation is continued for a period of several years. Unless time and funds are sufficient to permit the inclusion of a far larger number of cases within the total group handled than was feasible in the present instance, the exclusion of all cases who failed to complete the official schedule of tests not only means the loss of valuable data but is likely to reduce the number of cases so greatly that few reliable conclusions can be drawn from the results. Nevertheless, in spite of the changes in its personnel, we believe that the general character of our group has not shifted greatly in the course of the twelve-year period. From the beginning the children included in the growth study have come, on the average, from the more favored intellectual and social classes. The continued selective process that has caused the children of less intelligent parents to drop out of the group in greater proportion than those of the superior groups has been counterbalanced, to some extent, by the addition of new and more representative cases from time to time.

For the calibration of the scales and the preparation of tables for transforming the number of items passed into equally spaced units of measurement, we are indebted to

vii

Professor M. J. Van Wagenen of the department of educational psychology of the University of Minnesota, who is also chiefly responsible for the preparation of Chapter IV of this monograph. A word of explanation is needed in connection with this chapter. It now appears that the table of standards used by Professor Van Wagenen had the effect of concentrating the C-score values too closely about the mid-point of the distribution, with the result that the scores used in deriving the IQ-Equivalents yielded a distribution of considerably lower variability than what should automatically appear from the use of the formula given on page 44 if the SD value in terms of score points had been correct. Unfortunately, inasmuch as we had taken this value for granted until the greater part of the statistical work had been completed,* the correction of the error would have involved a recomputation not only of all the test scores for the individual children but also of practically all the statistical work already completed.

Meanwhile the desirability of utilizing terminal status as a criterion for item selection, as proposed by Anderson,† had become constantly more apparent to us. The growing body of evidence that the tests in present use for infants and young children yield only slight evidence of what their ultimate status is likely to be, suggests that our present methods of appraising early mental status may not be well chosen. Mrs. Maurer has accordingly undertaken the task of constructing a new scale by this method. As yet the work is not sufficiently far advanced to permit any statement about the success of the project, but the underlying theory seems essentially sound.

It was largely because of Mrs. Maurer's decision to develop this new scale that we decided against rescoring the original blanks to correct for the restricted variability just mentioned. Had the error been of a different nature, such a correction would have been imperative. As it is, we believe that it has had little, if any, effect on our findings because we have been concerned throughout the study with relation-

* It was, of course, immediately apparent that the variability of IQ-Equivalents for the cases included in the growth study was decidedly less than the 17.5 points assumed for the standardization group. However, because of the selected character of this group we had anticipated a fairly marked reduction in variability.
† See p. 16.

ships rather than with absolute values. The rank order of the cases is not affected in any way. The fact that the scores are expressed in slightly different units should have no effect on the validity of our conclusions, since the means for the different ages are correctly located and the restriction in variability does not affect the equality of spacing but merely assigns lower numerical values to the differences between individuals all along the line. The use of 17.5 as a measure of dispersion was arbitrary. Any other number would have served as well; the choice of 17.5 was determined by the desire to make the numerical distribution of IQ-Equivalents conform as closely as possible to that of the 1937 revision of the Stanford-Binet. Actually, as may be seen from Table 10, on page 57, the unit of variability is about .72 of that of the 1937 Stanford,* about .80 of that of the 1916 Stanford (Tables 19–21), and about .90 of that of the Arthur Performance Scale for children under the age of 10 years (Tables 30–32).

We have not changed the value of 17.5 used in the formula on page 44 in spite of the fact that our data do not conform to this distribution. Our reason lies in the fact that because the 1937 Stanford is likely to be the "standard" test for most purposes for some years to come, there is definite advantage, in our opinion, in utilizing this figure as a standard for the expression of intellectual deviation. In the meantime, if the national emergency permits, we hope to be able to present a revised table of IQ-Equivalents for the Minnesota scales, unless the completion of Mrs. Maurer's investigation renders it unnecessary for us to do so.

One further point should be noted. From the beginning of our work in testing we have made it an invariable rule that all retests shall be given without foreknowledge of the child's standing on previous tests, as far as this is at all compatible with the fact that during a part of this period only one psychometrist has been employed.† It is of course possible that

---

* Table 10 appears to show a slight reduction in the variability of the IQ-Equivalents with advancing age. This difference, however, does not appear in any of the results of the growth study. We are therefore inclined to attribute it to sampling differences.

† During the twelve-year period five different psychometrists were employed for periods ranging from one to three years each. Since tests were given annually, memory of the previous standing of a child cannot have operated to any marked extent because of the frequent change in examiners.

when a retest is given to a child by the same examiner who tested him a year previously, some impression of his former level of performance may have remained in the memory of the examiner, in spite of the fact that several hundred other children have been tested in the interim. Yet inasmuch as no examiner is ever allowed to look up a child's previous record before retesting we believe that the possibility of the differential handling of children on the basis of reputation has for the most part been eliminated.

The extent to which this factor has affected the correlation between tests and retests reported from other sources is unknown. It is, however, reasonable to suppose that an examiner who knows that a given child has previously earned a low IQ may be somewhat more ready to accept his "I don't know" as final or to pass on to a new item after a relatively short hesitation when a child is not expected to be able to pass the item in any case. On the other hand, when a child is expected to do well on the basis of previous performance, there is the likelihood that hesitations or refusals may be interpreted by the examiner as indications of reluctance rather than of inability. Urging or other incentives may then be employed in order to elicit the desired response. Since the precise amount and kind of urging permitted are rarely specified in the instructions for administering individual tests, the possibility that the examiner may vary the testing procedure in accordance with some previously formed estimate of the child's ability is a hazard even when she is not aware of the child's previous test standing. But the hazard is greatly magnified when she has this knowledge. To the extent that this has occurred some part of the correlation between test and retest may be regarded as spurious, since it results from examiner's attitude rather than from unmodified child behavior. We believe that the methods of control imposed in this study have largely, if not wholly, freed the data from errors of this kind.

F.L.G.
K.M.M.

CONTENTS

LIST OF TABLES

xiii

PART I
Construction of the Minnesota Preschool Scales

I. HISTORICAL SURVEY*

Although mental tests for school children first appeared shortly after 1900, those for preschool children are of more recent origin. The purpose of the early tests was to distinguish between feebleminded and normal children in school, in order that the feebleminded might be segregated and given special training suitable to their needs (Binet, 1905, 1908, 1911; Goddard, 1910, 1911a, 1911b). Once the usefulness of the tests had been demonstrated, the work was carried further: first, in the checking and revision of tests for school children; second, in the extension of the testing method to a wider age range. The First World War gave impetus to mental testing at higher age levels, particularly to methods of group testing, and the success of the army tests led to the development of a wide variety of group tests for adolescents and adults.

Since the war there has been a gradual recognition of the importance of the early years in the scientific study of behavior and of the need for more adequate methods of measuring children's abilities before they enter school. Up to that time the difficulty of securing the necessary number of subjects of appropriate ages had been a serious obstacle to normative studies of mental growth. However, the establishment of nursery schools and kindergartens in recent years has made large groups of children available for testing, and the literature written for parents has stimulated their interest in mental development and insured their cooperation. These trends have simplified the problem of finding subjects and have made it feasible to develop tests suitable for the younger age levels.

Tests for preschool children may be divided roughly into three groups: tests for infants, covering the prelinguistic period from birth to 18 months, tests for children of nursery school age, and tests for kindergarten children. In the sections that follow we shall discuss each of the three groups separately.

Tests for Infants

The first systematic descriptions of developmental changes

* Assistants in the preparation of these materials were furnished by the personnel of the Work Projects Administration, Official Project No. 165-1-71-124, Subproject No. 259.

in the behavior of infants are to be found in the observational studies of single infants made by many psychologists during the latter half of the nineteenth century and by a small number of individuals much earlier. The first such study to be preserved is Tiedemann's series of observations on his son, first published in 1787. Like that of Tiedemann, the studies made by the Sterns (1907, 1909, 1914), Preyer (1882), the Scupins (1907), Shinn (1900), and others, have attempted to include practically the entire field of infantile behavior. Others, either because of lack of time or because of more specialized interests, have confined their observations to more limited areas, such as the development of speech. The concept of mental testing was yet to be born, and none of these early investigators had more than a shadowy idea of what we now regard as normative standards of behavior. Nevertheless, frequent comparisons of the child's age at the appearance of a given form of behavior with the ages reported in other biographical records show that the possibility of a practical as well as a scientific utilization of their reports was gradually taking shape.

The earliest attempt at a truly systematic formulation of standards of early development that we have been able to locate was published in 1887 by S. E. Chaille (see also Goodenough, 1934). Although Chaille's study has heretofore attracted little attention, it is noteworthy as one of the first attempts to use the chronological age at which certain characteristic signs of development usually appear as a criterion by which the developmental level of individual children may be judged. His data are based on his own medical case records, which seem to have been unusually complete, and on reports of the development of individual children culled from the medical and psychological literature of the time. The normative standards that he presents for the appearance of a large number of physical and mental traits in many instances agree very well with the results of recent studies. He tends, however, to place reactions at earlier ages than do modern investigators, suggesting either that the observer was lenient in his judgment or that the infants he studied were somewhat precocious. It is possible that both of these factors were operative. Norms are given for each month during the first year and for 15, 18, 24, and 36 months.

In 1915 Sheffield published a list of activities that might be expected of the normal child at certain age levels. The list was designed chiefly to help the physician diagnose cases of feeblemindedness at an early age and thus served as a rough intelligence test.

The first formal tests for infants to attain widespread use were those published by Kuhlmann (1922), who revised the Binet-Simon scale by eliminating some tests, by shifting the position of others, and by adding tests to extend the scale at both the upper and lower levels. This test is still one of the most widely used of all those designed for infants. Kuhlmann has recently published a revision of his scale (1939), but as yet the new form has not been extensively used outside his own department.

Undoubtedly the most important study of infant behavior yet to appear is that carried out at Yale University under the direction of Arnold Gesell (1925, 1929, 1940). Although Gesell and his co-workers have not yet succeeded in assembling their findings into a fully standardized scale, their remarkably complete analyses of the manifold reactions of infants of varying ages to a great variety of stimuli have formed the basis of most of the tests for infants that have appeared since 1925. Their division of items into four major classes—motor, linguistic, adaptive, and personal-social behavior—is a distinct step forward. In the testing of older children it has long been realized that not all behavior is equally indicative of the quality known as intelligence. Probably the same principle holds good in infancy. If so, more careful distinctions among types of behavior are essential. Gesell's system of classification may not be precisely what is needed, but it is at least an effort in the right direction. The question of differential "patterns" of intelligence will be discussed later.

Linfert and Hierholzer (1928), under the direction of Furfey, drew extensively on Gesell's developmental schedules in devising their carefully standardized series of tests for the first year of life. Directions for administering and scoring the test items are very explicit. Norms based on fifty infant tests at each of six age levels—1, 2, 4, 6, 9, and 12 months—have been worked out in such a manner as to yield quantitative standards for each day of chronological age from birth to 12 months. By reference to these tables developmental ages and developmental quotients may be derived in the same way as the familiar mental ages and intelligence quotients used with older children.

Bühler's series of "baby tests" (1930, 1932, 1935) cover the age period from 1 month to 6 years. The suitability of these tests for American infants was studied by Herring (1937), who found a number of rather marked differences between the ages at which certain items were placed by Bühler and the ages at which they were usually passed by her own subjects. These tests are nevertheless of considerable interest because of the large number of items not commonly found in tests of American origin.

The California First-Year Mental Scale was developed by Bayley (1933) for use in a longitudinal study of the mental development of a group of sixty-one infants, followed from the time of birth to about 10 years. Like those in other American scales, the California test items are patterned largely upon those used by Gesell (1925). The unique feature of this scale is the fact that its standardization was based on the performance of the same group of children at successive ages, thus ruling out the possibility of sampling irregularities from age to age. The group studied is probably somewhat superior to the average of the general population. Once the degree of superiority is known, however, appropriate allowance for this factor can readily be made. This test will be considered further in the discussion of the prediction of later status from earlier status.

Shirley's (1931, 1933a, 1933b) very complete study of the development of a group of twenty-five infants during the first two years of life is also very suggestive for the student of mental growth. Although Shirley made no attempt to formulate a definite system of mental measurement, tentative norms for a large number of mental, motor, and personality items are presented.

Cattell (1940) has recently published a scale suitable for children of 3 to 36 months of age. This scale was planned as a downward extension of the 1937 revision of the Stanford-Binet, Form L (Terman and Merrill, 1937). From 22 months up Stanford-Binet items are used in combination with the other items, some of which are drawn from Gesell's work (1929, 1940) and some of which were devised by Cattell and her associates. The group used in the standardization of the scale, selected before birth on the basis of the mother's willingness to cooperate and the father's permanence of employment, has proved to be of superior mental ability (average IQ on the 1937 Stanford-Binet at 36 months is 118). Reliability coefficients, corrected by the Spearman-Brown formula, range from +.56 to +.90; the median coefficient is +.87. While this scale is too recent to have been tried out by other investigators, it appears to have certain advantages over earlier scales for the same age levels. The tests are arranged in an age scale, and procedures for administering and scoring are much more objective than those previously available.

TESTS FOR CHILDREN OF NURSERY SCHOOL AGE

The 1916 revision of the Stanford-Binet (Terman, 1916) included some tests for children of 3 and 4 years. Although these tests were originally intended for use with backward children of kindergarten and primary school age rather than for younger normal children, up to the last few years the great popularity of the Stanford revision for use with older children caused these tests to be adopted in preference to all others for use with nursery school children. One of the chief reasons for undertaking a revision of the scale was its recognized inadequacy outside the age range of approximately 5 to 13 years. At the older ages the standards proved to be too high, causing a spurious drop in the mean IQ for children beyond the elementary school range; at the lower ages, where the standardization was based on only a small number of cases, several items were misplaced as to range of difficulty, and the norms as a whole were so easy that the resulting IQ's were too high. A further source of error lay in the coarseness of the scale divisions at the lower ages. Since only six tests were provided for each year of chronological age, success or failure on a single item meant a difference of two months in mental age, which is approximately one third of a standard deviation of the entire distribution of mental ages for children of 3 and 4 years. Obviously the effect of chance errors was greatly magnified in the case of the younger children, where the denominator of the fraction used in computing the intelligence quotient ($IQ = MA/CA$) is small.

It was for the purpose of correcting these and other defects in the 1916 revision that Terman and Merrill (1937) some years later set about preparing a new and improved form of the scale, a task that required more than a decade to accomplish. The revised scale consists of two forms, each with a range of effectiveness from 2 years to the adult level. Between the ages of 2 and 5 years six tests are provided for each half-year of chronological age and six for each whole year thereafter. This gives finer distinctions at the ages where they are most needed. The lower age ranges of the scale, moreover, were planned with the interests and abilities of young normal children in mind, rather than those of older retarded children. As a result of this change in emphasis, the character of the tasks selected for those ages has been considerably modified. Tests using tiny toys that appeal to small children, pictures, and interesting tasks, such as bead-stringing and block-building, make up the bulk of the items, whereas the proportional number of purely verbal and abstract items is much reduced. This change in the manifest purpose of the tests is also apparent in the standardization procedure. The selection of cases was as carefully controlled at the preschool as at the school age levels; and the number of cases used, though smaller than at the later ages, was still large enough to yield reasonably stable norms. For the nursery school range approximately seventy-five children were tested at each half-year level.

The Kuhlmann revision of the Binet scale (1922), which was described in the section on tests for infants, has also been popular at the nursery school level. This scale provides eight instead of six tests for each whole year of age. A detailed critique of the preschool portion of this scale has been published by Goodenough (1928).

A scale for young children, designed on the point-scale principle instead of the year-scale principle, was undertaken as a supplement to the Yerkes-Bridges Point Scale (Yerkes and Foster, 1923). This scale was entitled the Infant Point Scale but was never tried on children below the age of 3 and was standardized only incompletely for children between the ages of 3 and 7.

The Merrill-Palmer series of tests (Stutsman, 1931) is made up largely of nonverbal tasks, although some tests involving the use of language are included. The tests in this scale are highly interesting to young children and have been standardized on a fairly large number of cases. Mental age norms, sigma scores, and percentile ranks for each raw score are available. Scoring is mainly in terms of time. The age range for which the test is designed is 18 months to 6 years. An unfortunate defect in the construction of this scale is the use of raw scores based upon a simple counting of items that are obviously quite unequally spaced with respect to difficulty. The tests themselves are arranged in approximate order of difficulty and are divided into groups according to the chronological age at which they are most frequently passed. No use is made of this grouping except as a guide to the range over which the testing should be extended. The number of items included at each half-year age level varies irregularly from three to fourteen, with the smallest number falling in the age range from 66 to 71 months and the largest in the range from 30 to 36 months. Inasmuch as each test carries equal weight in determining the score, inconsistencies in interpreting the numerical results are bound to occur, for if the age groups are correct, the amount of mental growth represented by success on a single item at different points on the scale does not correspond to any known theoretical curve of mental development. This irregularity is further reflected in the changes in the value of the standard deviations of scores from age to age, a fact that completely invalidates the IQ as a method of expressing the child's level of brightness. This point is discussed more fully in Chapter VII.

Another regrettable feature of these tests is their dependence on speed of response. Of the ninety-three test items* fifty-eight are scored in terms of time. Since young children have but rudimentary concepts of time and frequently refuse to be hurried when engaged in an interesting task, there is serious doubt as to the validity of the results of timed tests for this age range.

Stutsman does not report reliability coefficients for these tests. Kawin (1934) reported a test-retest coefficient of +.59 for 169 children. The interval between the two tests was 9.2 months. Driscoll (1933) obtained similar results with an in-

* A test item is here defined as any separately scored level of performance. Most of the timed tests are scored at several different levels, depending on the time required. Thus the Wallin Peg Board A Test counts as four test items, since credit is allowed for success at 38, 25, 20, and 17 seconds.

terval of 6 months between testings. In both these studies IQ's derived in the usual manner were used for computations.

The most recent study of the Merrill-Palmer scale is that of Wellman (1938), who has made an extensive analysis of test results for 281 children. Wellman compared results obtained by the use of IQ's, sigma scores, percentile ranks, and raw scores for the 510 Merrill-Palmer tests administered to her subjects and concluded that there is some inadequacy in the derivation of the raw scores affecting all the interpretative measures. In further analyses of her data she makes use of IQ's for ease of comparison with other studies reported in terms of IQ. For her subjects the Merrill-Palmer scores showed no relation to parental education or occupation, although Kuhlmann-Binet tests given to the same children at the same ages showed the usual relationship to both. Correlations between Merrill-Palmer and Kuhlmann-Binet IQ's ranged from +.45 to +.65 (with an interval of one week between testings). Prediction from an early test to a Stanford-Binet (1916) given at 6 or 7 years was higher for the Kuhlmann-Binet than for the Merrill-Palmer. Further discussion of the predictive value of these tests will be given in Chapter VII.

Atkins (1931) has devised a form-board test entirely nonverbal in nature, since the directions are given in the form of fore-exercises which do not require the use of language on the part of examiner or child. The test was devised for use with preschool children for whom verbal tests are not suitable because of foreign language background or deafness. It was standardized on 150 children divided into four groups with mean ages at 2, 3, 4, and 5 years. The sample was matched to the population of Minneapolis with reference to parental occupation and an effort was made to include as many different racial groups as possible. Correlations between the two forms of the test administered within a week's time range from +.79 to +.96; correlations between the Atkins Object-Fitting Test and the Minnesota Preschool Scales given at the same ages range from +.52 to +.85.

The California Preschool Mental Scale (Jaffa, 1934) includes items taken from most of the previously constructed infant and preschool scales. It consists of two forms and includes tests for children from 15 to 84 months of age. The tests are arranged in order of difficulty in ten categories descriptive of the type of task to be performed. This scale has been used principally for repeated measurements on various samples from the population of Berkeley, California, in connection with a series of research projects in progress at the University of California.

Other tests for children of preschool age that are less well standardized or have not been combined into scales are described in some detail in Stutsman's *Mental Measurement of Preschool Children* (1931). A complete bibliography of tests for infants and children under the age of 6 years has been prepared by Hildreth (1939).

TESTS FOR KINDERGARTEN CHILDREN

Many of the tests designed for children of preschool age and for children of school age may also be used with kindergarten children. The various revisions of the Binet-Simon scale are decidedly better adapted for use with children 5 years and older than for the younger ages. A third revision, the Herring-Binet (1922), can be used with children of 5 and older, though since the mental ages that can be earned on this scale start at 5 years it is not suitable for use with kindergarten children below average in ability. The author of this test claims that it has exceedingly high reliability and correlates almost perfectly with results obtained by the 1916 Stanford-Binet (Terman, 1916), but the findings of other investigators have been somewhat less favorable. However, since it has the merit of providing an additional test of the Binet type in which very few of the items exactly duplicate those included in either the Stanford or the Kuhlmann revisions, it will probably continue to find use as a check test, especially when there is reason to think that a child has received coaching on the forms that are more widely known.

Arthur (1930, 1933) has published a point scale of performance tests, calibrated in equal units by the discriminative-value method first devised by Arthur and Woodrow (1919). The tests used are taken over from a number of earlier performance scales, especially those found in the well-known Pintner and Paterson series (1917). The Arthur scale may be used with children as young as 5, though it is better suited to the first-grade level. The author claims that this scale "agrees almost as closely with either of the Binet scales (Stanford or Kuhlmann) as Stanford-Binet IQ's agree with retests on the Stanford-Binet scale." However, the statistical results of the standardization as presented in Volume II of the author's report (1933) do not entirely bear out this statement (see Chapter X). Nevertheless, the Arthur scale is undoubtedly useful as a rough means of evaluating the intelligence of children for whom, because of sensory or linguistic handicaps, other methods of testing are inappropriate.

[The Goodenough "drawing a man" test (1926) has certain points of convenience that recommend it for use when only a crude measure of intelligence is required. It is well suited to the kindergarten level and requires but a few minutes to administer and score.]In reliability and in correlation with other measures of intelligence it compares favorably with other group tests for young children. During the last few years this test has been used in several important racial studies with apparently good results.

A number of tests have been planned for use by teachers to determine the fitness of children for kindergarten or first-grade work. The most common of these are the Detroit Kindergarten Tests (Engel and Baker, 1921), the Rhode Island Kindergarten Test (Bird, 1923), and the Pintner-Cunningham Tests (1921). A new and extremely valuable development in this field is provided by the so-called readiness tests, which, although they correlate highly with the ordinary verbal tests of intelligence, are specifically designed to measure the child's readiness for formal instruction in school subjects. The Van Wagenen Reading Readiness Test (1932) and the Metropolitan Readiness Tests (Hildreth and Griffiths, 1933) are among the most carefully standardized.

PREDICTIVE VALUE OF TESTS FOR INFANTS, PRESCHOOL
CHILDREN, AND KINDERGARTEN CHILDREN

Although gross mental deficiency can usually be recognized, even without the aid of tests, before the end of the first year of life, attempts to predict future standing on the basis of infant tests have been disappointing. When tests designed for infants are repeated after an interval of a few days or even two or three months, a fair degree of consistency in the test-standing of individual children is usually found. But when unselected children first tested in infancy are retested some years later, little or no relationship between the results of the two series of measurements has been established. Surprisingly enough, a number of investigations have even suggested the possibility of a small negative correlation between standing on the tests now available for infants and later standing on tests designed for children of preschool age or older. Furfey and Muehlenbein (1932), for example, found small negative correlations ($-.11 \pm .13$; $-.34 \pm .11$; and $-.20 \pm .12$) between the developmental quotients earned on the Linfert-Hierholzer scale by three groups of infants first tested at 6, 9, and 12 months respectively and their 1916 Stanford-Binet IQ's earned at the age of 4 years.

Bayley (1933) found that the correlations between earlier and later measurements showed a consistent tendency to decrease, both as the interval between tests was increased and as the age of the child at the time of the first test was decreased. Thus the correlation between the average sigma score earned on monthly tests during the first three months and the average for the fourth, fifth, and sixth months was $+.57$. As the interval between tests was increased, the correlation with original standing steadily dropped. By the age of 18 months it had become slightly negative ($-.04$) and at the age of 3 years it fell to $-.09$. In this connection it is interesting to note that the correlations between the infant test scores and the education of midparent also show a tendency to be negative in sign up to the age of about 18 months, after which they become consistently positive, and by the age of 2 years they attain a magnitude comparable to that found for older children. Of the fifteen correlations reported by Bayley for ages ranging from 1 to 15 months, eleven are negative with values ranging from $-.01$ to $-.29$; three are positive, ranging from $+.03$ to $+.08$; and one is exactly zero. After the age of 15 months all the correlations are positive and of fair magnitude.

In Shirley's study (1931, 1933a, 1933b), probably because of the small number of cases included, the findings from age to age are somewhat less consistent, but here too the tendency toward a small negative correlation between the results of tests given during the early part of the first year and those given in early childhood is apparent. Although taken separately, each of these negative correlations is well within the limits of chance variation from zero; the fact that they appear in all of the major studies reported to date is very striking and merits further investigation.

An unpublished study by Conger* possibly throws light on the question. Using the Linfert-Hierholzer scale Conger tested twenty-five babies on each of two successive days at the ages of 1, 2, and 3 months, making a total of six tests for each infant. She found, as did Bayley, that the correlation between tests given on successive days increased with the age of the child and that the correlation between the tests given at 2 and 3 months was higher than that between tests given at 1 and 2 months or 1 and 3 months. No relationship was found between the scores earned by the infants and those earned by their mothers on either the 1916 revision of the Stanford-Binet or the Arthur Performance Scale. However, when the results of the infant tests were correlated with the length of time since the last feeding,† it was found that all six correlations were positive, ranging from slightly above zero to approximately +.5. This suggests that the placidity and drowsiness characteristic of the healthy, well-fed infant may be unfavorable to a good performance on the tests included in the infant scales and that children who are somewhat restless and uncomfortable may actually do somewhat better than those who are more calm and placid. If this is true, it is not impossible that the children of less intelligent parents, because they have poorer general care, may on the average be slightly more restless and alert at the time of taking the tests and therefore may respond somewhat better to the type of sensorimotor stimulation included in the infant scales. Such a condition, however, even if prolonged into later life, would not help the child to respond to the kind of items included in the scales for older children; thus the spuriously high ratings obtained in infancy would no longer be gained and the true mental status of the children would be revealed. This interpretation is of course largely hypothetical and later

* J. A. Conger, "An Evaluation of the Linfert Scale for Measuring the Mental Development of Infants." Unpublished M. A. thesis, on file in the Library of the University of Minnesota.

† The infants and their mothers were inmates of a maternity home for unmarried mothers. Feeding schedules were rigidly adhered to in all cases; hence the interval between feeding time and time of test could be ascertained with a high degree of accuracy.

investigations may show that chance alone provides the only explanation needed.

Early studies of the constancy of the IQ frequently included some cases first tested before the age of 6 years. Unfortunately the results of these investigations were rarely presented in such a form as to make it possible to study independently of each other the effect upon the stability of the individual IQ's of (1) the interval between tests and (2) the age at the time of the first test. Studies thus far available suggest that both age and interval play a part. In most of the results reported to date, the younger the child when first tested and the longer the interval between tests, the less stable the IQ's. Some of the more recent studies have controlled these factors more adequately than the earlier ones, but only a few have been based upon a sufficient number of cases or have covered more than a few years.

The children originally studied by Bayley (1933) have now passed their ninth birthdays and have been given, in addition to the infant tests devised by her, several testings on the California Preschool Mental Scale and on both the 1916 and 1937 revisions of the Stanford-Binet. From analysis of these additional data Bayley has concluded that prediction of a child's standing four or five years later cannot be made on the basis of tests given under 4 years of age (1939). In a recent article (1940) she has presented mental-growth curves for individual children that appear to show marked irregularity in mental growth.

A study in which both age at initial test and interval between tests have been taken into account is that of Honzik (1938), based on a large number of cases. Test results of 252 children from groups being studied longitudinally at the University of California at Berkeley were analyzed. The children were given several testings on the California Preschool Mental Scale throughout the preschool period, beginning at 21 months, and were subsequently tested on the 1916 Stanford-Binet at the ages of 6 and 7 years. Correlations between early and later test scores when the initial test was given before 3 years of age were too low to be of much value for prediction, but correlations from 3 years upward ranged from +.54 to +.76, increasing fairly regularly with age. By the use of an age ratio (CA first test/CA second test) Honzik showed constancy to be related both to the age at the time of the initial test and to the interval between the tests. The correlation between initial and subsequent tests, when the initial test was given at a relatively late age and a long interval elapsed before the retest, was shown to be about the same as that between tests when the initial test was given at a relatively early age and the interval was short. When the interval was held constant, the higher the age at the initial test, the higher the relationship of the initial score to the retest score.

Several investigators have recently become interested in the relationship between test-retest correlations and terminal status, with reference to the selection of test items to be included in preschool tests. In an article concerned with the limitations of infant and preschool tests Anderson (1939) has demonstrated by analysis of data from several sources, including Bayley and Honzik, that while test-retest correlations decrease as the interval between tests becomes greater when referred to initial standing, the relationship of each succeeding test to terminal status increases. According to Anderson, this is mainly due to the increasing amount of overlap in the functions measured. Children rarely lose what they have already attained in mental growth; as terminal status is approached, a larger portion of the complete growth is included in each succeeding measurement.

Anderson points out that though the traditional criteria for the selection of test items are (1) increasing scores with advancing chronological age, (2) correlation with ratings of intelligence, (3) correlation with academic record, and (4) internal consistency, actually only the first of these is consistently used in all scales. He discusses the need for including more than one criterion in the evaluation of items for mental tests if the accuracy of predictions based on such tests is to be increased and suggests that terminal status be one of these criteria. Since terminal status is, after all, what we are primarily interested in, it seems probable that its use as one criterion for the selection of items would materially increase accuracy of prediction. Use of the longitudinal method is obviously a necessary condition for applicability of this criterion. As stated in the Preface, an analysis of this type is already under way.

Studies reported up to the present time appear to warrant

the conclusion that tests given after 2 years of age have some significance in predicting the child's probable standing over a period of at least three or four years, but just how far into the child's future the predictive value of tests given at nursery school level may be said to extend is still a matter of inference rather than of exact knowledge. In this monograph the findings from a twelve-year study carried out at the University of Minnesota will be presented in the hope of providing further evidence on this important question.*

GENESIS OF THE PRESENT STUDY

In 1928 Goodenough published the results of a detailed study of the reliability of the Binet tests for children of pre-school age. For this she used the Kuhlmann revision (1922), which was at that time the only revision that included tests standardized for children below the age of 3. A total of 495 children ranging in age from 18 to 54 months were examined. From these children three groups of 100 each, whose chronological ages were 2, 3, and 4 years respectively, were selected for intensive study, selection being based on paternal occupation, sex, examiners, interval between tests, and degree of cooperativeness shown by the child during tests. These children were given two tests each, with an average interval of 5.9 weeks between testings.

The results of this investigation may be summarized briefly. The mean algebraic change (*i. e.*, taking account of of the plus and minus signs) in IQ from first to second test averaged +4.4 points and was greatest for the 4-year-olds and least for the 2-year-olds. Almost 4 per cent of all the children who were retested showed changes in IQ of 25 points or more. The tendency to gain in IQ was greatest for children whose fathers were engaged in some profession and least for those whose fathers were day laborers. On both tests the children from the upper occupational groups ranked distinctly higher than did those from the lower groups. When the individual tests were considered, it was found that many of them were misplaced in the scale and that the norms given by Kuhlmann for 2 through 4 years were somewhat too

---

* See also *Thirty-Ninth Yearbook of the National Society for the Study of Education* (*Intelligence: Its Nature and Nurture*) (Bloomington, Illinois: Public School Publishing Company, 1940), Part I.

lenient for this group. Further analysis of the results showed that nursery school attendance had no appreciable effect on changes in IQ.

These general conclusions were drawn by the author of this study (pages 126–28):

> Development probably proceeds more rapidly during the preschool years than at any subsequent period. . . . It is evident . . . that the tests at present available for use with young children are not sufficiently refined to render them serviceable for use in the solution of problems for which a high degree of precision of measurement is necessary. . . . It has been shown that inconsistencies in rating can be traced in large measure to certain individual test items. Other important sources of error are marginal successes and failures, incorrect placement of certain items and failure to secure a maximal response from the child, especially with respect to certain tests which have little intrinsic interest value for children at these ages. Defects of this sort can be corrected. Elimination of unreliable items and substitution of others less subject to modification through chance factors, the use of finer units of measurement, greater precision in the description of procedures and standards, and more consistent attention to the motivating power of the separate items as used with young children should bring about an appreciable improvement in the reliability of the scale.
>
> There seems to be no valid reason why it should not be possible to develop a series of tests which would measure intellectual status as accurately at the age of two years as at twelve or fourteen.

Starting with this point of view, the construction of a more accurate scale of tests for preschool children than had thus far been devised was undertaken. The investigation, which is now complete, has resulted in the development of a scale of high reliability which for purposes of finer analysis may be divided into two comparable subscales, one of a verbal and the other of a nonverbal type. Two equivalent forms of each scale are now available. An account of the process by which the scales were constructed is given in the succeeding chapters of Part I of this monograph. Part II presents the results of follow-up studies on children first tested on the Minnesota Preschool Scales, covering a period of twelve years.

II. STANDARDIZATION OF THE SCALES

The formulation and standardization of the Minnesota Scales for Preschool Children occupied about five years. As soon as the study of the Kuhlmann-Binet scale, mentioned in the preceding chapter, was completed, the construction of a scale to be used with children from the ages of 18 months to 5 years was begun. The earlier study had shown the necessity for careful selection both of the tests and of the children to be tested as well as the desirability of using more refined statistical methods in the compilation of results.

Much preliminary work was done in making the first selection of tests. The literature was combed with considerable care for tests that had been given to children of these ages, and every test that seemed at all promising was considered. Members of the faculty of the University of Minnesota who were or had been interested in the testing of young children were interviewed, and several new tests resulted from these informal discussions. Thus a fairly large number of test items was compiled. Each of these was tried out on from twenty to thirty children of the age for which it was judged to be diagnostic. Some of these were children enrolled in the University of Minnesota nursery school; others were children who had been brought to the Institute of Child Welfare for mental tests. The results obtained for each item were examined with care to determine which items should be retained in the main series to be tried out for final standardization.

Three criteria were used in discarding items: (1) the extent to which they differentiated between children whose ability was already known through other measures; (2) the objectivity of scoring, which was determined by having two experienced examiners score each test independently and then compare their ratings; and (3) the interest value of the material for children. Items to which any considerable number of subjects objected were discarded on the theory that unless a child likes and is interested in tests he will frequently not put forth his best effort. Others which, though not actually objectionable to the child, apparently failed to interest him were also dropped. This third criterion is obviously a subjective one, but since the examiners who were working on the tests had had considerable experience in testing young children, it was felt that their opinion was a better criterion of the child's interest than any other measure obtainable.

From the group of tests thus selected for further investigation, two forms were then prepared, Form A and Form B, each containing twenty-nine short series of tests. The two forms corresponded in the number and type of tests employed but differed in the details of the individual items. Since there is some evidence that repeated administration of one scale will improve a child's score through familiarity with the tests, it was thought desirable to use a second form of the scale when a child had already been given one form. With these two forms as material the main investigation was planned.

It was recognized at the outset that the scales thus devised were too long, and that in the final standardization some of the items would have to be eliminated. Since each form required approximately an hour's time for administration, restless children or those who were easily fatigued often had to be given a rest period before completing the test. One of the problems to be solved by the final standardization was how the tests could be shortened without material loss in accuracy.

PLAN OF THE INVESTIGATION

Experience has shown that a factor of great importance in determining the performance of children on mental tests is the socio-economic status of the family. It may be thought that if an investigator simply collects an enormous number of cases, he will obtain a sampling representative of the population at large. It has been found, however, that different classes of children predominate in the groups available at the different ages and that at all ages the extremes of the social distribution are easier to obtain than are children from the middle ranges. The more intelligent groups volunteer to have their children used as subjects; the lower classes can be reached through social agencies; but the middle groups must be particularly sought or few will be secured. In order to obtain a nearly representative group, the occupation of the father was used as the criterion of socio-economic status. The procedure employed by Goodenough in selecting cases for her study of the Kuhlmann-Binet scale was followed.* The cases

---

* This procedure involves classifying all occupations of adult males as listed in the census into six main groups when urban populations only are considered. These

were so chosen that each occupational group at each age contained the same number of boys and girls. When an odd number was necessary, balance was obtained in the succeeding group (see Table 1). Ages were taken to the nearest month. Exactly one hundred cases were used in each half-year age

TABLE 1.—OCCUPATIONAL DISTRIBUTION OF CASES USED FOR STANDARDIZATION AT EACH AGE LEVEL

Occupa-tional Group	Test Groups											
	A–B			A Only			B–A			B Only		
	Boys	Girls	Total	Boys	Girls	Total	Boys	Girls	Total	Boys	Girls	Total
I	1	0	1	1	1	2	1	0	1	1	1	2
II . . .	1	1	2	0	1	1	1	1	2	0	1	1
III . . .	4	5	9	5	4	9	4	5	9	5	4	9
IV . . .	3	3	6	3	3	6	3	3	6	3	3	6
V	2	2	4	2	2	4	2	2	4	2	2	4
VI . . .	2	1	3	1	2	3	2	1	3	1	2	3
Total	13	12	25	12	13	25	13	12	25	12	13	25

group. For the calculation of the norms on a first administration of Form A the first two groups were combined, giving for each chronological age the distribution shown in Table 2. Likewise the last two groups were combined in the calculation of norms for an initial administration of Form B. The standardization is thus based on a total of 900 children, 100 in each of the half-year age groups from 18 months to 6 years. Since half the children were given both forms, the number of tests used in standardization is 1,350.

In order to cancel the effects of practice, the order of giving

groups may be characterized as follows: I. Professional; II. Semiprofessional and managerial; III. Skilled trades, clerical and retail business; IV. Semiskilled trades and minor clerical; V. Slightly skilled trades; VI. Day laborers. For a complete list of the occupations included within each class see Appendix A of the reference cited (Goodenough, 1928).

It should be noted that this list includes only urban occupations, since the test was standardized wholly upon urban children. Because the upper occupational classes, especially Group I, are largely made up of urban residents and because it has been found that the average IQ of children from these classes is distinctly higher than that of children from the middle and lower groups, it is probable that our standards are somewhat higher than those that would have been obtained from a truly representative sampling of the entire population, including rural as well as urban children. Some allowance was made for this possibility by making the normative standards somewhat lenient, with the result that the mean IQ-E's for our standardization groups typically run slightly above 100. For a more complete classification of occupations based upon the census data for the entire country see Appendix A in *Experimental Child Study* by Florence L. Goodenough and John E. Anderson (New York: Century Co., 1931).

the two forms was experimentally controlled. Thus at each age twenty-five boys and twenty-five girls were given Form A first, and the same number were given Form B first. Of the children who were given Form A first, half were given Form B at a second sitting, usually on the following day, never

TABLE 2.—OCCUPATIONAL DISTRIBUTION OF CASES USED FOR CALCULATIONS OF NORMS AT EACH AGE LEVEL IN EACH FORM

Occupational Group	Boys	Girls	Total	% of Total	Cumulative %'s	Occupational Distribution, Twin Cities
I. . . .	2	1	3	6	6	5.4
II . . .	1	2	3	6	12	11.7
III . . .	9	9	18	36	48	49.0
IV . . .	6	6	12	24	72	73.3
V . . .	4	4	8	16	88	88.2
VI . . .	3	3	6	12	100	100.0

more than a week later. The same plan was followed with the children who were given Form B as the initial test. Thus fifty children, equally divided as to sex, were given Form A at their first sitting and twenty-five other children were given Form A not more than a week after they had been given Form B. The results of the tests given at the second sitting have been treated separately.

SOURCES FROM WHICH SUBJECTS WERE OBTAINED

When the Institute of Child Welfare was first organized at the University of Minnesota a certain number of parents promptly made application for their children to enter the nursery school. In our study these children were classed as *applicants*. Since the families in the lower occupational groups were much slower in asking for the privileges of the institute and since we desired contact with children from all classes, a systematic search was made for children of preschool age in the immediate neighborhood by means of a block survey. The children thus located were classed as *candidates*. In addition to these two sources, children were obtained from the public schools, parochial schools, orphanages, settlement houses (including both prekindergarten groups and day nursery children), and infant welfare clinics (including both the well-baby clinics, which are chiefly concerned with maintaining the health of children, and the preschool clinics, which are mainly habit clinics); a certain number of children had also been located in connection with another research project in progress at the institute.

The examiners who took part in the collection of the data for the scales were Dr. Florence L. Goodenough, who was in charge of the entire investigation, five young women who were her assistants,* and a number of graduate research assistants who had previously completed a course in mental tests for young children. These students had also had considerable experience in testing before taking this course. †

Most of the tests were given in the Institute of Child Welfare building, some in the settlement houses and clinics, and a very few in the homes of the children. The time of day for giving the tests was selected so as not to interfere with the child's regular schedule; that is, no child was tested at an hour when he usually slept or when the testing would postpone a meal.

Whenever possible the second form of the scale was given the day after the first form. The two were never given on the same day, and the interval between the administration of the two forms was never more than one week.

No observers were admitted to any of the examinations, and the mother was not allowed to be present except in a few cases in which the child became unduly disturbed at her absence and in which the testing procedure did not seem to be affected by her presence. Whenever the mother was present the fact was noted on the record blank.

No child's record was included in the standardization group unless it appeared to be a satisfactory one. The criterion of "satisfactoriness" was the behavior of the child as rated by the examiner immediately after the test. No child whose rating in the following scale fell below 3 in shyness or negativism or below 4 in distractibility was included in the standardization group. The system of ratings used is reproduced below.

SHYNESS

1. Child comes to examining room readily, talks freely, seems entirely at ease throughout test.

* Margaret Dickinson, Marjorie Armstrong, Helen Bennett, Louise Schmidt, and Josephine Conger.
† Dorothea McCarthy, Ella J. Day, Edna Kahlberg, Esther McGinnis, Emily Payetta, Florence Justin, Helen Brown, Hannah Faterson, Katherine Van Tuyl, Lucille Emerson, Lucille Hamilton, Marion Myers Jacobson, Eunice Snyder, Ruth Staples, and S. Margaret Light.

2. Child shows some hesitation at first but does not cry or seem frightened. After a few minutes' acquaintance is entirely willing to remain with examiner and appears to be completely at ease thereafter.

3. Child requires much persuasion before he can be induced to remain in room without mother. Eventually yields but continues to show some anxiety as to mother's whereabouts; has to be reassured frequently. May cry a little at the outset.

4. Child cannot be persuaded to remain in examining room without mother. With the mother present goes through the tests in a fairly satisfactory manner.

5. Child continues to cry or to cling to mother and cannot be persuaded to undertake the tests, even with mother present, or takes too few to justify a rating.

NEGATIVISM

(This may be an accompaniment of the behavior described under shyness, but it frequently occurs independently.)

1. Child is entirely obedient and docile throughout tests; is willing at least to attempt whatever he is asked to do.

2. Child offers minor objections to some of the tests but when urged and encouraged goes ahead with apparently undiminished effort.

3. Child requires much urging on any test that does not immediately appeal to his interest. May refuse flatly to try at first but objections can be overcome by subterfuge. Tests that arouse his interest are responded to readily.

4. Child shows a tendency to negativistic behavior on practically all tests. Even tests which attract his interest are likely to be performed opposite to instructions. Subterfuge, bribery, or special firmness has to be used throughout in order to obtain results.

5. Child refuses to perform any of the tests or undertakes too few to warrant a rating.

DISTRACTIBILITY

1. Child sits quietly during tests, pays good attention to directions throughout, is not unduly distracted by outside stimuli, and does not interrupt test with irrelevant remarks.

2. Child sits quietly during tests but is inclined to chatter on irrelevant subjects and is rather easily distracted by outside stimuli.

3. Child is somewhat restless, frequently climbing on table and attempting to handle material not then in use. Attention wanders easily but is also easily recalled.

4. Child is distinctly hyperactive, runs about the room, snatches materials, inquires into everything he sees or hears. Attention can be held only for brief intervals, but by being caught "on the fly" he can be made to go through the tests.

5. Child shows extreme hyperactivity. Attention span so brief

that he often loses track of what he is to do before completing a test. Results are too incomplete to warrant a rating.

Since it is quite possible that excluding from the standardization group those children who seemed uncooperative might involve some degree of selection along intellectual lines, every possible effort was made to reduce the number thus excluded. If a child seemed unduly shy or negativistic on his first visit, no attempt was made to test him on that day. Instead he was allowed to play about the examining room for a time so that he would become acquainted with the examiner and the room. Then the mother was asked to bring him back for a second attempt within a day or two. By employing this method, we reduced the number rejected because of poor cooperation to a very small percentage of the total. It is believed that any error of selection that may have been introduced in this way is at least far smaller than the error that would have resulted from including in the series a large number of records which were inadequate representations of the actual ability of the children concerned.

III. THE SELECTION OF THE TESTS AND THEIR ARRANGEMENT

In the selection of the tests for the Minnesota Preschool Scales it was natural that Goodenough's (1928) work on the 1922 Kuhlmann revision of the Binet should be given the greatest weight. However, other studies were reviewed with care and the final scale represents a combination of test items and ideas gleaned from many sources. There follows a detailed discussion of the selection of each of the tests included in the final scale.

POINTING OUT PARTS OF THE BODY

In almost all scales since the time of Binet, pointing out different parts of the body has been used as a test for very young children. In the Minnesota Preschool Scales the different parts of the body are to be indicated on a doll instead of on the child's own body. Experience has shown that some children are embarrassed or diffident about pointing out their own features, though they are willing to point to any part of a doll. The kind of doll appears to be immaterial providing it exhibits the parts of the body called for in the tests. A doll of approximately six inches in length was used in the standardization of the scale. Care was taken to select dolls with clearly defined ears and with legs that could be bent to a sitting position (see test 9, Form A).

POINTING OUT OBJECTS IN PICTURES

The idea for this test was taken from Kuhlmann (1922), although a different set of pictures was used. This performance appears to represent about the lowest measurable level of the vocabulary test. (For the modern child pointing to the objects themselves is but slightly easier, since pictures are so common a feature of his environment.) The child is able to point to pictures of familiar objects before he can call the pictures by name when they are presented; similarly he can name the pictures before he can answer questions such as "What is a dog?"

NAMING FAMILIAR OBJECTS

This test is closely related to the preceding one and has also been included in most of the revisions of the Binet scale.

The list of objects used in the Minnesota scales is a modification and extension of lists used in other scales.

COPYING DRAWINGS
Copying drawings has also been used in many scales. The drawings used in the Minnesota scales are variations of those used in earlier scales.

IMITATIVE DRAWING
This test is a variation of one in the Kuhlmann revision. It includes more models for drawing and uses a more precisely standardized procedure.

BLOCK-BUILDING
Gesell (1925) included block-building in his schedules. The Minnesota scales use block-building of several degrees of difficulty. The pyramids used in one form of the Minnesota scales are also used in the Merrill-Palmer Scale of Mental Tests (Stutsman, 1931).

RESPONSE TO PICTURES
The child's response to pictures is commonly used in Binet revisions. In some revisions the pictures used by Binet have been retained. Illustrations from *Jingleman Jack* have been substituted for them in the Goddard revision (1910), and the other scales have used pictures made especially for them. The pictures used in the Minnesota scales, selected from the catalogue of the Perry Picture Company, are as follows: No. 1064, *Kiss Me*, by Holmes; No. 1115, *Inquietude*, by Olivie; No. 908, *Shoeing the Horse*, by Landseer; No. 1120, *The Doll's Bath*, by Igler; No. 1061, *Family Cares*, by Barnes; and No. 887, *The Village Blacksmith*, by Herring. The method of selection was as follows: First, from the catalogue of the Perry Picture Company, fifty pictures were chosen that met the following criteria: (1) Each picture suggested a simple story and included familiar persons, animals, or both. (2) The persons or animals were engaged in some activity of interest to children. (3) The characters appeared in clear relief and therefore could be easily recognized. Complex pictures were avoided. On the basis of the combined judgments of a number of people experienced with the behavior of young children, two sets of six pictures each were se-

lected from this group of fifty pictures for actual trial. The basis of selection was as follows: Each picture contained at least three main objects (persons, animals, or such objects as a house, a flight of stairs, a chair) and showed a simple activity. Each set of pictures presented an apparent range of difficulty in regard to interpretation. For example, a series might include one picture showing a very obvious everyday activity, a second picture suggesting rather than showing such an activity, and a third including an activity likely to fall outside the child's personal experience but of a type that could be rather easily interpreted by inference. Each set of six pictures was tried out on groups of children of different ages; six were discarded and the remaining six paired for difficulty and type of performance elicited. One member of each pair, a total of three pictures, is used in each form of the scale.

KNOX CUBE IMITATION

Various investigators have used the cube imitation test first devised by Knox (1914). We have changed the material somewhat in the Minnesota scales by fastening the cubes to a strip of wood and by reducing the distance between the cubes to one inch. The cubes are painted bright red to add interest. The order of taps is taken from Pintner and Paterson (1917).

OBEYING SIMPLE COMMANDS

Many revisions of the Binet scale have used the obeying of simple commands as a test for young children. The Minnesota scales use one command, after Kuhlmann (1922), although the command is not the same. Tests involving two and three commands were tried out but were discarded in the final standardization of the scales.

COMPREHENSION

The comprehension questions used in the Minnesota scales are taken, with a few exceptions, from the Stanford (Terman, 1916) and the Kuhlmann (1922) revisions.

DISCRIMINATION OF FORMS

Tests for the discrimination of forms were devised by Kuhlmann (1922) and used by Terman (1916) with slight changes. We have added ten new designs to the ten used in these revisions, using five new and five old designs in each form.

Naming Objects from Memory

From the Kuhlmann (1922) scale we have taken the idea of naming pictures from memory and have extended the test by having the children name objects as well.

Recognition of Forms

The recognition of forms was taken over from the Kuhlmann (1922) scale, but with the size of the designs reduced, the instructions slightly varied, and the exposure time reduced to five seconds. In the final scale we have included only three designs to be recognized.

Colors

Naming colors has been a favorite test in many revisions of the Binet. The Minnesota scales merely use more colors.

Tracing a Form

Tracing forms was used by Kuhlmann (1922) and by other investigators, who used the Porteus (1915) mazes for this test. The Minnesota scales use three forms of increasing difficulty, with a new scoring system.

Picture Puzzles: Rectangular Series

Binet (1905) used the patience game, a fairly simple puzzle requiring that two triangles be put together to form a rectangle. Gesell (1925) made this puzzle more interesting by adding a picture to the cards. This also made it simpler by providing an additional cue for the matching. The idea of the test as it appears in the Minnesota scales, however, was taken from the Rossilimo series (1911), in which the pictures have a clear outline against a white background.

Incomplete Pictures

Various people have worked with pictures from which some part is missing. Gesell (1925) has the child complete an unfinished picture of a man. Other experimenters have been interested in the question of how complete a drawing must be in order to be recognized. The task of naming incomplete pictures included in our scales was taken over from Gesell

(1925), who makes use of a series of incomplete drawings of a watch. A large number of incomplete drawings were presented to intelligent adults. Those suggesting only one object to them were retained for trial with the children. A drawing of a circle, for example, could not be used because to a child it might suggest a ball, a saucer, or any number of different objects. On the other hand, it was necessary to make sure that the early drawings in the series were not too suggestive of the completed picture, or the value of the test would be lost. The seven series of incomplete pictures included in our scales, three in each form, plus a demonstration series, represent the best of the twenty or more that were tried out.

Digit Span

The digit span test has been much used and requires little discussion here. Because of its low interest value for young children we hesitated to include it, but its favorable showing by our other criteria induced us to use it. The time required has, however, been cut to a minimum by giving only as many of the three trials on each series of numbers as are required to determine success or failure.

Picture Puzzles: Diagonal Series

Diagonal picture puzzles are obviously more difficult than the rectangular type.

Paper Folding

Of a large number of paper-folding tests that were tried, only one satisfied our criteria sufficiently well to be included in the final scale. This test is more difficult than those in the Gesell (1925) or the Merrill-Palmer (Stutsman, 1931) scales and the scoring is rather lenient.

Absurdities

Absurdities have been used in many scales. The easy absurdities in these scales were taken in part from those suggested by Yerkes and Foster (1923) and were in part original with us. The more difficult ones were taken from the Stanford revision (Terman, 1916).

Mutilated Pictures

This test is a variation of the incomplete picture test in which the child is to point out the missing part of the picture.

Vocabulary

Most revisions of the Binet test have used a graded classification of the definitions given by a child as an indication of
his mental development, with definitions in terms of *use* considered the simplest type of answer. We included such a test
in the preliminary series of tests tried out for the Minnesota
scales, with these three possible levels of success: (1) definitions in terms of some fact regarding the object, such as its
use, its color, its structure; (2) definitions using "thing" as
genus with a qualifying phrase as above, or definitions giving
a more exact genus without a qualifying phrase; (3) definitions stating an exact genus with a qualifying phrase.

We found, however, that within the age range tested, very
few definitions falling into either of the last two classes were
given. We also found little evidence that statements about
the use of an object are more elementary than any other simple statements about objects. The lowest level of response is
evidently that of simply repeating the words "A cat is a cat"
or pointing and saying "That is a pencil." The next higher
response is, according to our data, a statement about the
object, whether it be of color, use, or some fact such as
"Water is wet." The test, then, at these early ages resolves
itself simply into one of vocabulary. We have abandoned
it as a separate test and added the most diagnostic words to
the vocabulary test. The other words included in the vocabulary test of the Minnesota scales have been taken from the
Stanford revision of the Binet scale (Terman, 1916). The first
twenty-five words of the Stanford revision were tried out and
those showing no consistent advance with age or those for
which the scoring was too subjective were eliminated.

Giving Word Opposites

In the test requiring the child to give the opposite of the
word spoken by the examiner we have followed the general
procedure of the Kuhlmann scale (1922), though the words
are not in all cases the same as those used by Kuhlmann.

Imitating Position of Clock Hands

Imitation of the position of the hands of a clock is a test
invented by a 4-year-old girl, one of the children used in the
preliminary trial of the test material. The child had hit upon

this device for telling her mother the time when the mother was too busy to go to look at the clock herself. The mother remarked to the investigators that it had interested her to find that whereas the child had no difficulty in showing how the hands looked when they were on opposite sides of the dial, she frequently became confused in trying to reproduce the positions when they were both on the same side. We decided to try the imitation out with other children and obtained such satisfactory results that we have included it in the scale.

Speech

Although Kuhlmann and Gesell have used speech as an indication of the development of the very young child, the Minnesota scales are, we think, the first to consider the vocal responses made by the child in the course of the examination worthy of ranking as a *separate* test.

Discarded Tests

The tests that were discarded are perhaps as important from some points of view as those that were retained. In the first place, several tests were discarded on the basis of the data obtained in the earlier study of the Kuhlmann scale (Goodenough, 1928). We felt that those tests had been tried out sufficiently to warrant their exclusion. Others were given a trial and eliminated because they failed to meet one or another of our criteria. Binet (1905) used a test of esthetic comparison in which the child was asked to state which of two pictures was prettier. The pictures in the Pintner-Cunningham group test (1923) were tried out for this purpose, but in the final formulation of the scale we abandoned this test, since our results seemed to indicate that chance is a major factor in determining the choice at all ages up to 5 1/2 years.

We also attempted to devise a simple test involving the reproduction of the thought of a passage, such as those used in Binet revisions. For this purpose we used very short stories in which the children showed considerable interest, but unfortunately the interest frequently did not reach the point of arousing in the child any desire to reproduce the story himself. The test as thus arranged also took a greater amount of time for administration than it appeared to deserve.

Two types of copying designs were also tried. In one the child was asked to string beads according to a given pattern. The other, which involved an arrangement of parquetry blocks, resembled in some respects the Kohs block-design test (1920). These design tests, however, proved to be greatly influenced by home and kindergarten experience. The children who were accustomed to these materials at home gave a performance markedly superior to that of children to whom the material was unfamiliar. Other tests that were discarded in the final standardization were the test of comprehending instructions at the eight-year level from the Kuhlmann scale (1922), which proved to be too difficult for all but a few of the brightest 5-year-olds and was much disliked by most of the children, and several paper-folding tests that aroused negativism in the younger children. Most of the tests that were retained have been shortened by eliminating the less satisfactory items.

ARRANGEMENT OF SCALES

As mentioned in Chapter I, there has been a generally recognized need for both verbal and nonverbal scales. This need is especially great at the preschool level because the wide age range at which speech develops in different children sharply limits the applicability and value of any test that is exclusively verbal or nonverbal. A number of scales of each type have been developed; but if two completely separate scales are used, the effect of practice is unequally divided because one of the two is given first. In the Minnesota scales verbal and nonverbal items are irregularly alternated, so that the effect of practice is equalized. Since the scores for verbal and nonverbal items are placed in separate columns the two scales are kept separate.

It has been customary to arrange the items of a point scale in order of increasing difficulty. We have followed this practice only to a limited extent. The main criteria observed in arranging the items were (1) to give variety to the tasks so as to increase their interest for the children and in so doing to intersperse those tasks of lower interest value, or those not involving the manipulation of concrete materials, with those that usually aroused much interest and (2) to obtain an approximate alternation of verbal and nonverbal items.

The printed materials of the Minnesota Preschool Scales are assembled in manila envelopes bound together like the pages of a book. This arrangement eliminates hunting for misplaced materials while the child fidgets and it keeps the materials out of sight when they are not in use. Labels containing the directions for administering each test are pasted on the appropriate envelopes, so that the examiner may refresh his memory by glancing at them. This does not, of course, excuse the examiner from becoming thoroughly familiar with the material and the procedure before attempting to give the tests.

The revised Manual (1940) includes a discussion of the conduct of examinations of young children as well as directions for the administration and scoring of each series of tests included in the scales. Nonverbal, verbal, and total scores, given in terms of C-scores, per cent placements, and IQ-Equivalents for each age from 18 to 71 months, may be read from the tables in the Manual.

IV. DERIVATION OF THE SCALE VALUES*

THE MEASUREMENT OF DIFFICULTY

In the earlier scales for measuring mental ability the mental year, or the amount of change in mental ability corresponding to a yearly change in chronological age, was used as the unit of measurement. No consideration was given to the fact that the mental year might vary at different levels of chronological age. The usual method of scoring, which takes as a basal age the year at which all the tests are passed and adds to that basal mental age a proportionate number of months for all tests passed above it, implies an equality in the mental year throughout the age range covered by the scales. It also assumes that all tests would have been passed below the basal mental age. Neither of these assumptions, of course, is necessarily true. In order to avoid these two sources of error, a measure of the variability of the age groups—the semi-interquartile range—was adopted as the unit of measurement in the construction of the Minnesota scales. Thorndike (1904) has shown that a measure of variability is a reasonably valid unit in which to express amounts of mental ability among older children. In view of the close conformity of the distributions of mental ability at higher ages to a normal surface of frequency, it seemed more reasonable to assume a similar form of distribution of mental abilities at lower ages than to assume any other form of distribution.

Although the number of cases† used at each half-year age level for determining the difficulty of the tasks was only fifty, the care with which the fifty cases were selected insured a closer approximation to a normal distribution of mental abilities than would be obtained with a much larger number chosen at random. The number of children successfully completing each task was converted into a percentage of the total number tested at that age, and this percentage in turn was

---

* The work of scaling was carried out by Professor M. J. Van Wagenen of the University of Minnesota, who is also responsible for the preparation of this chapter. The critical reader will note certain discrepancies between the use of the term *normal distribution* as found in this chapter and conventional practice. See Preface.

† This includes only the children who were given each form for the first time. An additional twenty-five subjects at each age were given a second form within a week after the first form had been used. For further information regarding the subjects and their selection, see Chapter II.

35

converted into a quartile value and expressed in tenths of a quartile, with the median of the half-year age group as the point of reference in each of the nine consecutive half-year age groups. As each task was done successfully by children in several successive half-year age groups, although of course by smaller and smaller proportions at decreasing ages, the difficulty of each task could be determined with greater stability by bringing all the quartile difficulty values to the same point of reference and averaging them.

The procedure thus consisted of finding the quartile value of each individual task for all age groups in which the degree

TABLE 3.—METHOD OF TRANSFORMING "PER CENT PASSING" INTO EQUALLY CALIBRATED QUARTILE UNITS

Age in Years	No. Succeeding	% Succeeding	Quartile Deviation Value*	Mean Difference Between Successive Ages	Deviation Referred to Median of 2-Year Group
2 6		12	+1.742	. . .	1.742
2 1/2 . . . 14		28	+0.864	1.1	1.964
3 31		62	−0.453	1.0	1.647
3 1/2 . . . 41		82	−1.357	1.2	1.943
4 48		96	−2.597	1.1	1.803
					1.82 (av.)

* From Fullerton and Cattell (1892, p. 16).

of success was greater than 1 per cent and less than 100 per cent, using for this purpose the Fullerton and Cattell table (1892, p. 16). The mean difference in terms of quartile values between successive age groups was then ascertained by averaging the differences in quartile values found for all tasks on which each of the two groups to be compared achieved partial, but not complete, success. In referring the quartile scores to the medians of the youngest age group, the differences in quartile value between the successive ages were added to the quartile values of the items as computed from the percentage passing them at each age. The following example, which illustrates the procedure for finding the difficulty value in quartile units of nonverbal item 13, Form B, will make this clear.

Table 3 should be read as follows: The first column lists the age levels at which some children, but not all, succeeded with the item in question. The second and third columns show the number and percentage passing this item out of the fifty children at each age who were given it as a part of the initial test. The fourth column shows the quartile-deviation value of each of these percentages in a normal distribution as given by Fullerton and Cattell (1892, p. 16). In column 5 the mean quartile differences between successive age groups, found by averaging the quartile differences on all the items of the scale, are given. In column 6 the values of column 4 are referred back to the median position of the youngest age group by adding (algebraically) the accumulated differences shown in column 5 to the quartile values given in column 4. The five approximations thus obtained are then averaged in order to cancel out, in part, the inconsistencies due to differences in the sampling of subjects at the successive ages.

It is unnecessary to present all the computations for the separate items in detail. It is sufficient to say that the high degree of stability in the difficulty values, when calculated from various points of reference, that is shown for the single item upon which Table 3 is based, was shown by practically all items eventually retained in the scales. A few items yielded inconsistent values; these were discarded on the assumption that the discrepancies were due to factors other than intellectual ability that operated unequally from age to age. Some evidence that this assumption was warranted was indicated by the fact that in many instances the discarded items were those that examiners found difficult to score uniformly or that varied greatly in their appeal to the children. It was also noted that a number of the discarded items had to do with specialized information or skills in regard to which unequal experience on the part of the children might readily bring about discrepancies in performance. We therefore felt warranted in utilizing the *consistency of scale placement* of an item, as reckoned from different points on the growth curve, as one criterion for its retention.

The results of the scaling procedure thus point to a high degree of stability of task difficulty for young children, just as has been repeatedly found for older children in the case of attainment tasks. At the same time the use of averages computed from several age groups tends to smooth out any variations from a reasonably close approximation to a normal distribution that might result from the use of only fifty cases for each distribution. Actually, of course, each scale value has been established on the basis of results from 250 to 350 cases, numbers that have been found to give a reasonably high degree of stability to the measurement of task difficulty.

SELECTION OF ITEMS FOR RETENTION IN THE FINAL SCALES

After the scale values for the tasks had been established, the next step was the selection of tasks for each of the four scales, two verbal and two nonverbal. The tasks were separated into verbal and nonverbal items on the basis of manifest language requirement. In making up the equivalent scales of both types, it was considered best that tasks equivalent in content as well as in difficulty be selected. While the function measured by either type of scale cannot be defined in terms any more precise than that each measures the functions of which the tasks are samples, it can be assumed that the equivalent scales (both verbal and nonverbal) measure the same functions, an assumption that is true only when the tasks are equivalent in content as well as in difficulty.

In making the final selection of tasks from the much larger number that had proved significant, three criteria were set up: (1) The equivalent scales should contain tasks of similar content. (2) The tasks in each scale should progress by equal steps—one-tenth of a quartile—as far as such tasks were available without violating the first criterion. (3) When more than one task was available for a given interval, the selection should be made on the basis of (a) comparative interest value for children, as judged by examiners experienced in using the tests, (b) dissimilarity to other items in the scale, and (c), most of all, the extent to which the items differentiated between children of the same age who did well or poorly on the series as a whole.*

The unusual care with which the tests were originally selected and the adequate preliminary tryout of the tasks in each test made it possible to select two equivalent scales of each type that met the first criterion perfectly and the second

---

* It will be recalled that similar criteria had already been applied in the selection of items to be tried out in the preliminary form of the scales. Hence in effect the application of criterion (3) involved a second weeding out of items by a more rigid application of the same principles that had previously been used.

and third criteria adequately. Occasionally a task had to be selected that would vary from the desired scale difficulty by one tenth or two tenths of a quartile, but very seldom was the variation more than two tenths. When variation occurred in one direction, a task varying in the opposite direction would be selected within a short interval. In this way the average difficulty values for consecutive groups of tasks were kept at the desired distances apart.

For the equivalent forms of the verbal scale two groups of eighty tasks each were selected, beginning with a task that approximately 50 per cent of 21-months-old children could do successfully and ending with tasks that only a very small percentage of 5 1/2-year-old children were found able to do.

For the nonverbal scales, tasks were not available at the early age levels.* The simplest task in each scale was passed successfully by 50 per cent of children at about 28 months of age. Hence the scale is somewhat shorter, consisting of fifty-five tasks instead of eighty, and cannot be used with very young children.

TRANSFORMING RAW SCORES INTO C-SCORES

The mathematical basis for the procedure used here was first suggested by Kelley in connection with scales for measuring spelling ability and was later used by him in constructing the Alpha and Beta Language Completion Exercises (1916). A variation of his procedure has been used here. Inasmuch as the tasks on each scale are equally spaced for difficulty, it becomes possible, by referring to a table of the probability integral, to ascertain from the number of items passed, the difficulty value of tasks for which success might be expected in 50 per cent of the cases.† This unit, known as

---

* Although a fairly large number of easy nonverbal tasks had been included in the original selection of items, unfortunately too few of these met the final criteria to warrant extending the scale to these ages.

† That is, if a large number of tasks of the same level of difficulty had been provided, a child whose C-score falls at that level would be expected to succeed in half of them. Since the test has been scaled in units of one tenth of a quartile, a gain of 10 C-score points at any level represents an increase in ability corresponding roughly to the difference between being able to succeed with 75 per cent of a set of tasks and being able to succeed with 50 per cent. In like manner, if two children of the same age earn C-scores that differ by 10 points, the brighter one would be expected to pass 75 per cent of a series of tasks of a level of difficulty such that the more backward child would pass only 50 per cent. Conversely, if a harder set of tasks is selected, of a level of difficulty 10 C-score points above the first, the brighter child would pass 50 per cent, whereas the more backward one would succeed in but 25 per cent. At a difficulty level 20 C-score points above the original series, the brighter child would

the C-score, has the merit of equal spacing of intervals and can therefore be used for computational purposes without violation of mathematical principles. For convenience a table of C-score equivalents for each number of items passed on the Minnesota Preschool Scales is presented in the Manual of Directions. It should be noted further that since the IQ-Equivalents (described in Chapter VI) are derived directly from the equally spaced C-scores, these values also are equally spaced, for they are actually standard scores that have been transmuted into units showing a distribution that corresponds roughly to that of the familiar IQ derived by dividing the mental age by the chronological age. Either the IQ-Equivalents or the C-scores may therefore be used in computation.

Accuracy of the C-Score Values

A number of rather exacting criteria were applied to the C-score method of determining an individual's level of performance. The first criterion was that of ascertaining whether the expected frequencies of success on tasks at different distances from the scores corresponded reasonably closely to actual frequencies of success in a large number of cases. This correspondence has been found to be reasonably close in a number of achievement scales (Van Wagenen, 1925).

In Table 4 are given the theoretical frequencies for each one tenth of a quartile from the theoretical frequency of 50, representing the child's score, and the corresponding actual frequencies based on one hundred scores ranging from C-scores of 105 through 117. The group includes twenty-five scores of bright children of ages 3 and 3 1/2 years on Form A of the verbal scale, twenty-five scores of a similar group on Form B, twenty-five scores of somewhat backward children of ages 5 and 5 1/2 years on Form A, and twenty-five scores of a similar group on Form B.

---

pass approximately 25 per cent of the tests and the more backward one 9 per cent. The C-score is thus based upon two well-known principles of mental development: (1) the fact that as tests are made more difficult fewer and fewer of them will be passed, and (2) the fact that, as has repeatedly been shown, the distribution of mental abilities conforms fairly closely to the normal probability curve.

Inasmuch as zero difficulty is an indeterminate point, the scale values do not start at zero. In the Minnesota Preschool Scales the point of reference has been so assigned that the average child of 18 months will have a C-score of 50. The average child of 45 months will have a C-score of 100 and at the age of 72 months the average C-score will have increased to 127.

Even when the scores of gifted children of a lower chronological age are combined with similar scores of less gifted children of a higher chronological age, the average difference between the theoretical and actual frequencies within a range of four quartiles for a group of only one hundred cases is less than 3.6 C-score points and is no greater toward the extremes than at the center of the distribution of successes.

TABLE 4.—CORRESPONDENCE BETWEEN THE THEORETICAL AND ACTUAL FREQUENCIES OF CORRECT RESPONSE AT EACH ONE-TENTH QUARTILE FROM THE C-SCORES MADE BY 100 CHILDREN

Distance from C-Score	Theoretical Frequencies to Nearest 0.1%	Actual Frequencies of 100 Cases	Distance from C-Score	Theoretical Frequencies to Nearest 0.1%	Actual Frequencies of 100 Cases
−2.5	95.4	95	+ .1	47.3	47
−2.4	94.7	100	+ .2	44.6	49
−2.3	94.0	95	+ .3	42.0	33
−2.2	93.1	93	+ .4	39.4	51
−2.1	92.2	92	+ .5	36.8	35
−2.0	91.1	94	+ .6	34.3	26
−1.9	90.0	97	+ .7	31.9	41
−1.8	88.8	98	+ .8	29.5	25
−1.7	87.4	93	+ .9	27.2	36
−1.6	86.0	94	+1.0	25.0	21
−1.5	84.4	90	+1.1	22.9	23
−1.4	82.8	89	+1.2	20.9	18
−1.3	81.0	73	+1.3	19.0	14
−1.2	79.1	84	+1.4	17.2	18
−1.1	77.1	77	+1.5	15.6	18
−1.0	75.0	78	+1.6	14.0	14
− .9	72.8	82	+1.7	12.6	13
− .8	70.5	75	+1.8	11.2	9
− .7	68.1	67	+1.9	10.0	12
− .6	65.7	66	+2.0	8.9	10
− .5	63.2	65	+2.1	7.8	8
− .4	60.6	60	+2.2	6.9	10
− .3	58.0	61	+2.3	6.0	6
− .2	55.4	55	+2.4	5.3	4
− .1	52.7	46	+2.5	4.6	4
0.0	50.0	46			

A second test is whether the probable error of measurement is practically the same toward the beginning, in the middle, and toward the end of the scales. In the present scales it has been found* to be 2.8 C-score points at each of these sections.

A third and more exacting criterion is the test of whether different sections of the scale will yield approximately the same score. When the C-scores were determined for the fifty

* By Otis formula, $PE_{meas} = \sqrt{2MD}$.

cases in the 3–3 1/2-year age group on the basis of tasks 11–40 in Form A of the verbal scale (when the tasks were numbered in order of difficulty), the median C-score was 97.8 units. When determined on the basis of tasks 41–70, with no overlapping of tasks, the median C-score was 99.7 units. The difference of 1.9 points is less than the probable error of the difference between the median C-scores. When the same procedure was carried out for the fifty cases in the 5–5 1/2-year age group, with the tasks likewise numbered in the order of their difficulty, the median of the C-scores based on tasks 21–50 was 124.8 units, whereas that of the C-scores based on tasks 51–80 was 124.3 units.

INTERPRETATIVE UNITS: IQ-EQUIVALENTS AND PER CENT PLACEMENT

Because the C-score units that serve as the basis for scale calibration are not universal measures but apply only to the particular scale for which they were derived, some method of expressing these scores in terms of units that have a more generalized meaning is essential. Two measures, known as the *per cent placement* and the *IQ-Equivalent*, have been used for this purpose. The first of these has been employed chiefly in educational measurement. It has the merit of being easily understood by persons with little or no statistical background, since it means simply the percentage of the difference between the most backward and the most advanced child likely to be found in a representative group of a thousand children of similar age. For example, if the C-score that is likely to be made by the most backward member of a representative group of a thousand children of the age in question is 55, whereas that of the most advanced case is 115,* the difference between these extremes is 60 points. A child with a C-score of 75 is 20 units (75 minus 55), or 33 1/3 per cent of the total range of his age group, above the position of the most backward member of this group. His per cent placement (taken to the nearest whole number) would therefore be 33.

A word of explanation is perhaps necessary to clarify the difference between the term *per cent placement* as here used and the more familiar *percentile rank*. If the distribution of

---

* Needless to say, these are theoretical values rather than values computed upon an actual sample, inasmuch as the latter would be based upon only two cases and would therefore be highly unreliable.

abilities conforms approximately to the well-known normal curve, the differences (in terms of score values) between successive percentiles or percentile ranks will of necessity be unequal, because percentiles represent successive equal segments of the *area* of the curve above the base line. Since the height of the curve decreases steadily toward the extremes, equal areas can only be maintained by including longer and longer segments measured on the base line as the extremes of the distribution are approached. Because of this inequality of score values, percentiles cannot be handled by the ordinary types of statistical computation. They cannot be added, subtracted, averaged, or subjected to other ordinary arithmetical processes without first being converted into other units. The per cent placement, on the other hand, is a linear measurement, marking off equal *distances* along the base line of the curve, and may therefore be handled like any other series of numerical values. The difference between the two will be easily kept in mind if we remember that the percentile or the percentile rank represents *equal areas above the base line,* whereas the per cent placement represents *equal linear distances along the base line.*

The IQ-Equivalent is merely a standard score in which the constants have been chosen in such a way as to make the numerical results correspond fairly closely to the already familiar IQ.* The assumptions involved in deriving the IQ-E's are fewer and easier of fulfillment than are those for the IQ derived by the usual method. Most people who have dealt with modern methods of mental measurement are familiar with the practice of reducing all scores to similar values by substituting a constant value of 50 for the mean score of a specified group and adding or subtracting from this assigned mean the number of standard deviations by which the individual surpasses or falls short of the mean of his group multiplied by 10. The formula thus becomes:

$$\text{Standard score} = 50 \pm 10\frac{x}{SD},$$

where x/SD equals the difference between the individual score and the mean score of his age group divided by the standard deviation of the group.

* See Preface.

Our procedure is the same except for the use of different constants, as shown below:

$$IQ\text{-}E = 100 \pm 17.5\frac{x}{SD}.$$

Because the IQ has attained such widespread usage among practically all persons dealing with test results, it has seemed desirable to provide a method of expressing test results in terms that are already familiar. The conventional method of obtaining the IQ, however, has both practical and theoretical disadvantages. From the standpoint of test construction there is the requirement of standardizing the scale over a much wider range of ages than that within which it is to be used, because the spread of mental ages so greatly exceeds that of the chronological ages in any group. If mental ages are to be used in finding the IQ, a test designed to have a range of usefulness for children from 2 to 6 years and for IQ's from 50 to 150 must actually be standardized on children from 1 to 9 years of age.* Furthermore, in the latter method the assumption is that the abilities and experiences of children outside the age limits of the test are qualitatively like those of children within such limits, an assumption that becomes increasingly hazardous as ages decrease. The most serious hazard in the ordinary method of deriving the IQ, however, is the mathematical necessity for maintaining the standard deviations of mental ages at a constant ratio to the chronological ages. Unless this is done the IQ will not have a constant meaning from age to age.† The fact that the IQ has been used in connection with many tests for which this condition is not met undoubtedly accounts in part for the wide discrepancies in individual standing often found on different tests of mental ability.

The choice of constants for the mean and standard devia-

---

* There is, of course, no possible method of standardization that frees the investigator from the necessity of including in his test enough items of suitable range of difficulty to sample the abilities of all children, both bright and dull, within the age range in question. Our procedure, however, unlike the mental-age method, does not require the use of subjects beyond the age limits of the test for purposes of standardization.

† For a further discussion of this point see Chapter VII. The extent to which failure to meet this requirement may vitiate test results has recently been demonstrated by Goodenough in an article entitled "Studies of the 1937 Revision of the Stanford-Binet Scale: I. Variability of the IQ at Successive Age-Levels," which will appear in a forthcoming issue of the *Journal of Educational Psychology*.

tion is arbitrary. The use of 50 and 10 in the more conventional procedure was dictated by practical convenience in computation. Our choice of 100 and 17.5 was based upon the desire to make the IQ-E's derived from the Minnesota scales correspond roughly in numerical value to those obtained from the 1937 revision of the Stanford-Binet.*

RELIABILITY OF THE SCALES

Table 5 shows the correlation between the C-scores on Form A and those on Form B for the standardization group. Fifty cases are included at each age level. The interval between testings ranged from one to seven days.

TABLE 5.—CORRELATIONS BETWEEN C-SCORES ON FORM A AND FORM B FOR THE STANDARDIZATION GROUP OF 50 CASES AT EACH AGE

Age in Years	Verbal Scale			Nonverbal Scale			Total Scale*		
	r	SD†	PE of Individual C-Scores‡	r	SD†	PE of Individual C-Scores‡	r	SD†	PE of Individual C-Scores‡
1 1/2 . .	.88	10.6	2.3	. . .	. . .	. . .	.88	10.6	2.3
2	.92	13.1	2.5	. . .	. . .	. . .	.92	13.1	2.5
2 1/2 . .	.90	10.6	2.3	. . .	. . .	. . .	.90	10.6	2.3
3	.85	11.7	3.1	.82	11.0	3.1	.89	10.9	2.4
3 1/2 . .	.80	9.3	2.0	.83	10.3	2.9	.86	10.0	2.7
4	.82	9.6	2.7	.91	9.0	1.8	.90	9.1	1.9
4 1/2 . .	.82	11.6	3.3	.77	9.7	2.7	.85	11.0	2.9
5	.89	11.0	2.5	.84	10.9	2.9	.90	11.0	2.3
5 1/2 . .	.85	10.1	2.6	.70	10.5	3.9	.87	9.9	2.4

* Total score = $\dfrac{2 \text{ verbal C-score} + \text{nonverbal C-score}}{3}$.

† In C-scores.

‡ Probable error of an individual C-score = $.6745\ SD\ \sqrt{1-r}$.

THE TOTAL SCALE

It will be seen from Table 5 that the self-correlations for the verbal scale run on the average slightly higher than those for the nonverbal scale and that the probable errors of measurement for the latter tend to be somewhat higher. Also nonverbal tests have been thought by many to be less significant indices of the level of development of the so-called higher mental processes than of the "simpler" sensorimotor processes, such as those used in the early and unsuccessful attempts at mental testing carried out by Cattell and others

* See Preface.

about the turn of the century. For these reasons it was decided to give more weight to the verbal scale than to the nonverbal in deriving a total score. Since the correlations between the two scales at the various age levels run for the most part between +.70 and +.80, which when corrected for attenuation become +.80 or more, the effect of differential weighting is less marked than it would be if the intercorrelations of the two were lower. Because the lack of a criterion made it impossible to use multiple correlation to determine the optimal weighting, it was decided to assign double weight to the verbal score. The formula used for finding the total or combined C-score is therefore:

$$\text{Total C-score} = \frac{2 \text{ verbal C-score} + \text{nonverbal C-score}}{3}$$

As will be shown in Part II, more recent findings based upon follow-up tests of the same children over a period of years have given reason to doubt the superiority of the verbal scale over the nonverbal, as was first thought to be the case. It seems probable, in view of our present findings, that the latter merits at least equal weighting with the former. It has not, however, appeared to us worth while to rework the data on the basis of equal weighting, particularly in view of the fact that a more drastic revision of the scales on the basis of an item analysis in which terminal, rather than initial, status is used as a criterion is now in progress.*

Relation of IQ-E on the Minnesota Scales to Socio-Economic Status

Table 6 shows the mean IQ-E's earned on each of the three scales by the standardization group. Both initial tests and retests (the latter corrected for effect of practice †) are included. The cases are classified according to paternal occupation. The data presented in this table were first worked out separately for ages and sexes. Forms A and B were also treated independently. Inasmuch as no consistent differences

---

* See Chapter VI.

† Because previous practice has been shown to affect practically all mental test results, particularly at the early ages, a correction for this factor is needed. By comparison of scores on first and second tests, it was found that two C-score points should be subtracted from the score earned on the second occasion in order to equalize the results.

appeared beyond the fluctuations to be expected from the small number of cases in each group, the results have been combined to show the general trend.

Examination of Table 6 reveals two significant points. First, there is the fact that on each of the scales a steady decrease in mean IQ-E is evidenced in passing from the upper to the lower occupational groups. This is entirely in accordance with the findings from other investigations in which the

TABLE 6.—MEAN IQ-E's ACCORDING TO PATERNAL OCCUPATION*

Scale	Occupational Group					
	I	II	III	IV	V	VI
Verbal	111.1	110.0	107.1	104.0	101.5	97.8
Nonverbal. . .	111.3	110.1	104.9	99.8	98.5	95.5
Total.	111.2	110.0	106.4	102.6	100.5	97.0

* Total number of tests included in table, 1,350; total number of children tested, 900. For distribution by paternal occupation, see Table 1, page 21.

same system of classifying occupations has been used (Goodenough, 1928; Terman and Merrill, 1937). The regression of IQ-E upon paternal occupation is, surprisingly enough, somewhat more clearly shown in the nonverbal scale than in the verbal scale. The second point of significance is that the mean IQ-E's for the total group run slightly in excess of 100. This is, of course, not accidental. Because our standardization group was drawn from a population that in all probability is somewhat superior to the average (the mean IQ on standard tests for Minneapolis public school children in the elementary grades is approximately 104), it was thought desirable to make our standards conform roughly to those obtained by other scales rather than to fit them rigidly to a sample from a population that is probably somewhat superior to the generality of urban groups and is almost certainly superior to the population as a whole.*

The marked difference in mean IQ-E between the two extremes of the occupational distribution that appears even at these early ages shows the importance of paying careful attention to the sampling of subjects used in deriving any test

* For a group of three hundred similarly selected preschool children who were given the 1922 revision of the Kuhlmann-Binet tests the mean IQ was 106.3. Most authorities, however, regard the standards for the early levels of this test as slightly too lenient.

norms which are to be used as standards of comparison for the performance of other children.

In this connection it is well to point out the rather obvious fact that the use of the Minnesota scale with rural children is not to be recommended, at least not until its suitability for this purpose has been experimentally demonstrated. It has not been feasible for us to test a sufficient number of rural children living at some distance from a large town or city to determine whether or not their performances on the scales would show either qualitative or quantitative differences from those of the urban children used in standardization. For this reason it seemed better to us to use only an urban population for standardization purposes in order that there should be no question as to the kind of population to which norms should be applied. The inclusion in our group of the small number of rural children that it would have been feasible to obtain would merely have rendered the test less suitable for urban children, without adding materially to its usefulness for rural children.

PART II
The Prediction of Later Status from Earlier Status

V. SOME THEORETICAL CONSIDERATIONS AND THEIR PRACTICAL IMPLICATIONS

The study of human mental growth is a task beset with many difficulties. Of the two possible approaches to the problem, the first, which has been most commonly employed in the past, consists of selecting a fairly large number of cases at successive age levels and applying to these cases whatever tests or other measuring devices are regarded as valid indices of mental differences within the area selected for study. This procedure, known as the *cross-sectional* method, is dependent for its validity upon several assumptions: that the sampling of children at each age is representative of a series of populations similar to each other in all respects except age; that the present findings for each of these groups would be duplicated (within the limits of the probable error of measurement) by the next younger group if the latter were examined after the appropriate interval of time; and that a group now at a more advanced level formerly occupied the same position as that now held by the particular age group being considered. The second procedure, known as the *longitudinal* method, involves the repeated examination of the same children at appropriate intervals.

It should be noted that, as ordinarily employed, neither of these methods is truly continuous. Each involves a sectioning of the growth stream at certain selected points and a comparison of the findings thus obtained with those from earlier and later levels. Each method has certain advantages and each is fraught with hazards of its own. The longitudinal method, which for the most part is a comparatively recent development in group studies, is regarded by many as greatly superior to the ordinary cross-sectional study. Shuttleworth (1939) has shown that as far as growth in height is concerned, the number of longitudinal cases required to yield a stable curve is far smaller than when the successive measurements are taken on different children.

Nevertheless, the advantages of this method are not as simple and unequivocal as many have assumed. Were it possible to maintain contact with all members of the original group from the beginning to the end of the study, many of the difficulties inherent in the practical application of such a procedure would disappear. But with conditions as they are, many cases are eliminated from the group as the experiment progresses, with the result that after this selective process has gone on for a period of years the cases finally available for continuous study are likely to differ from the original population in many respects, the nature and extent of which can be only partially surmised.

A further complicating factor in the longitudinal study of mental growth is the effect of practice in taking tests. Here one must choose between two evils. On the one hand there is the danger of simple learning effects when the same tests are repeated year after year. On the other hand there is the danger of differential content when new tests are substituted. Moreover, the effects of practice are not wholly eliminated even when tests of apparently quite dissimilar content are employed on successive occasions. There is no question but that habituation to the test situation itself constitutes a significant part of the practice effect, over and above any similarity in the measures used. This is particularly true when the subjects are small children.

These and other factors must be kept in mind in all interpretations of the results of repeated testings of the same subjects. We must not forget that our interest lies, not in the particular score earned on a given test at a given time, but rather in the inferences as to the child's probable level of response *outside the test situation* that we may justifiably draw from this score. If the factors that have just been pointed out affect the test scores to a different degree or in a different manner from one occasion to another, the real significance of correlation or absence of correlation between these scores is uncertain. Perseverational factors, leading to simple repetition of a response formerly given, may bring about a closer resemblance between test scores than that manifested in intelligent behavior in daily life. Differentials of cooperation and general adjustment may lower the correlation between tests far below the corresponding relationships in general behavior. Chance factors obviously affect both the correlations between tests and the correlations between general behavior on different occasions, and in any limited population even presumably random influences may show a systematic trend. It is necessary, therefore, to bear in mind continually that predicting a subsequent test score is not necessarily equivalent to predicting the level of behavior of which the score is presumed to be an index.

In the chapters that follow, the results of a twelve-year study of the development of children who were given either Form A or Form B of the Minnesota Preschool Scales as an initial measurement* of mental level are presented. The results of earlier tests have been compared with those obtained at later ages both on the Minnesota scales, within the age range for which it is suited, and on the Merrill-Palmer tests, the Arthur Performance Scale (Form I), and the 1916 and the 1937 Stanford revisions of the Binet scale. Illustrative case reports are included in order to show the possibilities and limitations of such studies, as well as some of the hazards of too literal interpretation of our present attempts to measure so tenuous and uncertain a function as the mentality of a young child.

* It is of course possible that some of these children had been previously tested by some agency other than our own. Certainly the number of such cases would be small, since none of the children had entered school or kindergarten at the time the Minnesota tests were administered. Children known to have had a previous test have not been included.

VI. RELATION BETWEEN EARLIER AND LATER STANDING ON THE MINNESOTA PRESCHOOL SCALES

THE IQ AND PREDICTION

In few areas of psychological investigation are the problems of measurement so closely bound up with the problems of prediction as in the study of mental development during childhood. Undoubtedly, the widespread attitude that mental measurement is chiefly for the purpose of prediction is a direct outgrowth of the fact that mental tests were originally devised, and have been chiefly used, as bases for practices involving the handling of children over extended periods of time. Unless it could be demonstrated that the tests were measuring something that was sufficiently stable to persist throughout the allotted time period, these devices would be of little service in planning long-time training programs for individual children.

The traditional uses of tests in selecting children for placement in institutions for the feebleminded or in special classes in the public schools, and as aids in solving problems of adoption or questions of vocational or educational guidance, all carry the implicit assumption that from the results of early tests the mental status of a child at a later age may be predicted with considerable accuracy. That this assumption is not wholly unwarranted when the first tests are given after the period of early childhood is past has been thoroughly demonstrated by many studies that are too well known to require enumeration. Even tests given during the preschool years have been found to have some positive value for prediction, though the amount of confidence to be placed in such predictions is considerably less than when the tests are given at a later age.

When this fact first became evident it was assumed by many that errors unrelated to the purpose of the tests provided a sufficient explanation for the lowered relationship between initial tests and retests. Shyness, failure to put forth real effort, resistance to the examiner, and similar emotional factors, also the fact that the items included in the tests for young children are qualitatively different from those employed at later ages, have been mentioned as sources of error. That these factors play a highly important part is unquestionably true, but the recent findings of Bayley (1940), Honzik (1938), Brown (1933), and others, as well as the data to be reported here, provide fairly convincing evidence that this is not the whole story. As Hildreth (1926) pointed out many years ago, the quotient method of specifying test results, useful though it may be as a practical device for showing the *average* rate of mental development of an individual over a period of years, tends nevertheless to cover up whatever fluctuations in rate of growth may have occurred. During early childhood, when the life span is still short and development rapid, the averaging procedure does not conceal these fluctuations so effectively because of the comparatively narrow base afforded by a low chronological age. Fluctuations in rate of development that are real but temporary may then operate to yield a fictitious estimate of the subject's most typical rate of development over a longer period of time, just as a small sample is less likely, other things being equal, to yield a dependable estimate of the characteristics of a total population than a larger sample.

PREDICTIVE VALUE OF THE TOTAL MINNESOTA SCALE

It was shown in Chapter IV that when the testings were separated by an interval not greater than one week, the cor-

TABLE 7.—CORRELATIONS BETWEEN IQ-E'S ON TESTS GIVEN AT DIFFERENT AGES AND AFTER VARYING INTERVALS OF TIME (TOTAL SCALE)

Age in Months		N	SD	r	PE
At Initial Test	At Retest				
Under 36 . . . 36–47		130	11.70	+.45	.05
Under 36 . . . over 47		135	11.05	+.53	.04
36–47 . . . . . over 47		241	11.65	+.67	.02

relations between Form A and Form B of the Minnesota Preschool Scales were encouragingly high. Table 7 shows that when this interval is increased to a year or more, the relationship is considerably less close.* This is quite in accordance

* In this and the following tables based upon the Minnesota Preschool Scales no distinction has been made between Form A and Form B. In repeated testings the two forms were used alternately.

with the findings of previous investigators on other tests. It is also apparent from Table 7 that even within the preschool period there is a tendency for the magnitude of the correlations between tests to increase with age at the time of testing.

Tables 8 and 9 compare the distribution of children from the various occupational classes in the standardization group with that in each of the three retested groups included in Table 7. Table 10 compares the means and standard deviations of the initial IQ-E's of the retested groups with those of the standardization group.* It is apparent from these tables that although the standard deviations have been only slightly narrowed, the total distribution has been moved several points up the scale of IQ-E's. The mean IQ-E of the total standardization group on the initial test was 102; within the selected portion of this group that was available for retest the mean initial IQ-E was 110. Only 6 per cent of the standardization group came from families in the professional group, whereas 37 per cent of the retested cases were classed at that level.

It is sometimes valuable to know not merely the degree of correlation between earlier and later testings but also the actual amount of variation in IQ-E that is likely to occur. Tables 11 and 12 show the distribution of changes for each of the three retested groups. Table 11 presents the actual distribution of these changes; Table 12 shows the percentage of each group for whom there occurred changes in test standing as great as, or greater than, the various stated amounts. The average change, disregarding sign, was 13.2 IQ-E points for the group under 36 months of age at the time of the initial test, 11.3 for the group between 36 and 47 months, 9.8 for the group over 47 months, and 10.7 for the total of 506 retests.

PREDICTIVE VALUE OF THE VERBAL AND THE NONVERBAL SCALES CONSIDERED SEPARATELY

It will be recalled that the items of the Minnesota scale have been classified into two subscales for which differential scores have been derived. Those items that demand a verbal response from the child or those that do not require a verbal response but in which success is nevertheless chiefly dependent upon the comprehension of verbal instructions (such as

---

* See Preface.

TABLE 8.—OCCUPATIONAL DISTRIBUTION OF CASES IN RETEST GROUPS AND
STANDARDIZATION GROUP

Test Group	Occupational Group					
	I	II	III	IV	V–VI	All Occu-pations
Standardization group .	54	54	324	216	252	900
Retest groups*						
Under 36 mos. . . .	45	22	26	23	14	130
36–47 mos.	50	25	25	21	14	135
Over 47 mos.	93	40	58	29	21	241
All retest groups . .	188	87	109	73	49	506

* Age at initial test.

TABLE 9.—OCCUPATIONAL DISTRIBUTION OF CASES IN RETEST GROUPS AND
STANDARDIZATION GROUP (IN PERCENTAGES)

Test Group	Occupational Group				
	I	II	III	IV	V–VI
Standardization group . .	6.0	6.0	36.0	24.0	28.0
Retest groups*					
Under 36 mos.	34.6	16.9	20.0	17.7	10.8
36–47 mos.	37.0	18.6	18.6	15.5	10.4
Over 47 mos.	38.6	16.5	24.1	12.0	8.8

* Age at initial test.

TABLE 10.—MEAN IQ-E'S AND STANDARD DEVIATIONS OF STANDARDIZATION AND
RETEST GROUPS (TOTAL SCALE)*

Test Group	Mean IQ-E	*SD*
Standardization group		
Under 36 mos.	102.1	14.1
36–47 mos.	103.5	12.9
Over 47 mos.	101.2	11.9
Retest groups		
Test under 36 mos.;		
retest at 36–47 mos.	108.4	11.7
Test under 36 mos.;		
retest over 47 mos.	108.7	11.1
Test at 36–47 mos.;		
retest over 47 mos.	111.0	11.7

* The figures given are the means and standard deviations on the initial test in
each case. The values given for the standardization group are the means and standard deviations of Forms A and B combined, since no distinction was made between
the forms on retests.

Table 11.—Distribution of Changes in IQ-E from Initial Test to Retest

Age in Months at Initial Test	N	Losses						Gains								
		−25 to −29	−20 to −24	−15 to −19	−10 to −14	−5 to −9	−4 to +4	5 to 9	10 to 14	15 to 19	20 to 24	25 to 29	30 to 34	35 to 39	40 to 44	45 to 49
Under 36	130	1	3	7	8	11	23	28	11	25	8	4	0	1	0	1
36–47	135	2	3	2	15	23	25	22	18	15	7	3	2	1	0	0
Over 47	241	0	1	12	28	36	58	47	26	17	12	4	0	0	—	0
Total	506	3	7	21	51	70	106	97	55	57	27	11	2	2	0	1

Table 12.—Cumulative Percentages Showing Probability of Gains or Losses Exceeding a Given Amount (Based on Table 11)

Age in Months at Initial Test	N	Losses as Great as or Greater Than:						Gains as Great as or Greater Than:								
		−25 to −29	−20 to −24	−15 to −19	−10 to −14	−5 to −9	−4 to +4	5 to 9	10 to 14	15 to 19	20 to 24	25 to 29	30 to 34	35 to 39	40 to 44	45 to 49
Under 36	130	.8	3.1	8.5	14.6	23.1	17.7	60.1	38.5	30.0	10.8	4.6		1.5		.8
36–47	135	1.5	3.7	5.1	16.1	32.9	18.3	49.6	33.6	20.4	9.5	4.4	2.2	.7		
Over 47	241	—	.4	5.5	17.2	32.3	24.4	44.5	24.8	13.9	6.7	1.7				
Average	506	.6	2.0	6.2	14.4	28.4	21.2	50.4	31.0	20.0	8.6	3.2	1.0	.6		.2

pointing out parts of the body) make up the verbal scale. The nonverbal scale includes items which not only demand no verbal response but in which the difficulty of performance is so much greater than the difficulty of understanding the instructions that success or failure rarely hinges upon the level of verbal comprehension.

Table 13 shows retest correlations of the verbal and nonverbal scales for the cases included in Table 7. As was to be expected, the retest correlations for the two subscales are consistently lower than those for the total scale. However,

TABLE 13.—CORRELATIONS BETWEEN IQ-E'S ON TESTS GIVEN AT DIFFERENT AGES AND AFTER VARYING INTERVALS OF TIME

Age in Months		N*	SD	r	PE
At Initial Test	At Retest				
		VERBAL SCALE			
Under 36	36–47	130	12.40	+.39	.05
Under 36	over 47 . . .	135	11.25	+.40	.05
36–47	over 47 . . .	241	10.70	+.55	.03
		NONVERBAL SCALE			
Under 36	36–47	54	13.65	+.43	.08
Under 36	over 47 . . .	65	15.20	+.54	.06
36–47	over 47 . . .	241	15.35	+.55	.03

* The nonverbal scale does not yield scores below 30 months of age; as a result there was a smaller number of cases in the earliest age group (under 36 months) than was available for comparisons of the verbal and total scales.

examination of these tables reveals a somewhat unexpected trend. Since the verbal scale is weighted twice as heavily as the nonverbal scale in determining the total score* and since the self-correlations of the former were consistently higher than those of the latter (in the case of the standardization group), it seemed reasonable to anticipate that the retest correlations after a period of time would also be higher for the verbal than for the nonverbal scale. Surprisingly enough, this is not the case. In two of the three comparisons the nonverbal scale shows a closer correspondence between initial test and retest than does the verbal scale, while in the third instance the correlation is equal. Apparently, from the standpoint of its predictive value over a period of time, the nonverbal scale is at least as good a measure as the verbal scale. It will be

* It will be recalled that this procedure was followed because of the higher reliability coefficients found for the standardization group (see pp. 45–46).

shown later that when the comparison is made over much greater time intervals and some other well-known test is used as the second measure, the nonverbal scale still shows itself to be as good or better a predictive device than the verbal scale.

This conclusion is quite contrary to our original expectation but it is a fact of much significance for the research worker who is interested in developing tests for young children. If our findings are sound, they suggest that the difference in the apparent character of the nonverbal material used in tests for young children, as compared with the predominantly verbal types of test commonly employed at later ages, is a matter of less importance than might at first be thought. Anderson (1939) has suggested that if we accept the point of view that the prediction of later mental status is a major aim in the construction of tests for young children, the best single criterion for determining the validity of any test item is its correlation with *terminal* mental status, rather than such immediate and circumstantial factors as internal consistency or correlation with other indications of ability obtained at the time. The assumption that the measure which best meets the immediate criteria will also best meet the test of time is here shown to be of questionable validity. Certainly the evidence available at the time of standardizing the Minnesota scales pointed to the conclusion that the verbal scale was the better of the two subscales. Nevertheless, the data just presented, as well as those to appear in subsequent chapters, suggest that the contrary may be the case. It should be noted here that the equality or possible superiority of the nonverbal scale is attained in spite of the fact that it contains only fifty-five items, whereas the verbal scale has eighty items. Because of the nonhomogeneous nature of these items we are not warranted in applying the usual statistical measures to determine the degree of improvement to be expected if the nonverbal scale were increased in length to equal the verbal scale, but it is safe to assume that some degree of improvement could thereby be accomplished.

RELATIONSHIP OF SEX AND SOCIO-ECONOMIC STATUS TO PREDICTION

Table 14 shows that when the initial tests were given before the age of three, the correlations between earlier and later testings were consistently higher for girls than for boys on both of the subscales as well as on the total. When all the children were at least 3 years of age at the time of the first test and 4 or older at the time of the second test, only the total scale showed a slight and unreliable advantage in predictive value for the girls. Although it is of course possible that the scales are somewhat better adapted to the interests and abilities of little girls than to those of little boys, it seems more probable that the sex difference in predictive value is a function of the well-known greater psychological and emo-

TABLE 14.—SEX DIFFERENCES IN CORRELATIONS BETWEEN EARLY
AND LATER TESTS

Age in Months		Boys			Girls		
At Initial Test	At Retest	N	r	PE	N	r	PE
		VERBAL SCALE					
Under 36	36–47 . . .	54	.33	.08	76	.41	.06
Under 36	over 47 . . .	68	.20	.08	67	.56	.06
36–47	over 47 . . .	119	.57	.04	122	.54	.04
		NONVERBAL SCALE					
Under 36	36–47 . . .	22	.29	.13	32	.50	.09
Under 36	over 47 . . .	34	.48	.09	31	.69	.06
36–47	over 47 . . .	119	.55	.04	122	.54	.04
		TOTAL SCALE					
Under 36	36–47 . . .	54	.30	.08	76	.53	.06
Under 36	over 47 . . .	68	.38	.07	69	.63	.05
36–47	over 47 . . .	119	.62	.04	122	.72	.03

tional maturity of girls during the early years. Further evidence derived from other scales will be presented in the following chapters.

The data have also been carefully examined to see whether the predictive value of the scales varies with the socio-economic level of the children, but no indication of such a trend could be discovered. The restriction in range of talent that results when the children of only a single occupational class are considered has the expected effect of lowering to some extent the median correlations between initial test and retest. There is also, of course, much greater variation from one coefficient to another as a result of the small number of cases in each class, but there is no indication that the test is better adapted to children from one extreme of the occupational distribution of the Twin City population than to those of another. It therefore seems unnecessary to present these figures in detail.

Discussion

In agreement with the findings of other investigators, it has been shown that the test performance of children first examined before the age of three years (that is, between the ages of 18 and 35 months) is a decidedly fallible index to their later standing on the more advanced items of the Minnesota Preschool Scales. The relationship is nevertheless sufficiently high to be worth taking into account. In terms of the index of forecasting ability, obtained through the formula

$$\text{Index}_{fa} = 1 - \sqrt{1 - r^2},$$

a prediction based on the test results alone is shown to be from 12 to 33 per cent better than a random guess, depending on the age of the children at the first testing and on the length of the interval between tests. Nevertheless, marked changes in standing occur in individual cases and these changes are decidedly more frequent than is likely to be the case when older children are used as subjects. In a comparison of 506 tests and retests, ten children, or approximately 2 per cent of the total, lost as much as 20 IQ-E points, and forty-three, or approximately 8.6 per cent, gained 20 points or more. The frequency of changes (either plus or minus) of this magnitude is at least five times as great as has usually been reported for children of school age.

Three factors appear to contribute to the lower predictive value of tests for very young children. Briefly stated, these are as follows:

1. *The greater difficulty of arousing and holding the child's interest in the tests and of motivating him to do the particular thing required by the test, rather than something else that may make a greater appeal to his fancy.* As Heidbreder (1924) has shown, children under 5 years of age are rarely interested in problem-solving as such. Their criterion of success or failure is internal rather than external. Success to the 3-year-old means the fulfillment of his own desires; it has nothing at all to do with the attainment of a goal set by an outsider or the solution of a problem just for the fun of solving it. Thus one of the most dependable sources of motivation for older chil-

dren is practically nonexistent at the early ages and no wholly satisfactory substitute for this direct interest in problem-solving for its own sake has ever been discovered.

2. *Differences in the overt character of the test items used at widely separated ages.* This may, and probably does, make for some degree of psychological dissimilarity in the functions measured on the two occasions. If this is true, irregularities in the individual measurements are almost inevitable, regardless of the actual form of the mental-growth curve. We have shown that in spite of their lower reliability at the time of measurement, the nonverbal scales predict later standing as well as, or possibly somewhat better than, the verbal scales. This suggests that a definite improvement in our present methods of testing young children may be effected by means of the analysis now in progress in which later standing on tests of recognized validity is used as the criterion for retention or nonretention of an individual item in the scale.

3. *Recent evidence indicating that individual curves of mental growth are in all probability far less even and regular than many have supposed.* Much of the known stability of the IQ's of older children can be accounted for as follows:

Apart from the comparatively rare instances of deterioration from disease or accident affecting the nervous system, actual loss in mental stature probably does not occur in childhood.* The denominator of the fraction used in computing the IQ includes both the age previous to the time of the first measurement and the gain in age during the interval between measurements. This makes for an artificial smoothing of the growth curve and a consequent correlation between earlier and later measurements, since if the two tests are truly measures of the same thing the second measurement includes the first. A correlation between the two is in effect a correlation between a whole and one of its parts; its magnitude will be affected by (1) the proportion of the whole that is included within the part originally measured, (2) the correlation between the original part and the increment, and (3) the ex-

---

* Children may, of course, fail to make measurable gain, with the result that their *intelligence quotients* become progressively lower, but it is very doubtful if *mental ages* truly decrease (except in pathological cases) before the period of mental senescence is under way, just as it is unlikely that physical height, once attained, will be truly lost, although, as the result of a given child's failure to grow, his small stature becomes increasingly apparent as he grows older.

perimental error of measurement, which, it should be noted, may differ for the two measurements. The first factor obviously depends on the age of the child at first testing and the interval between the tests, the third can be determined with fair accuracy by the appropriate statistical procedures, but the second has thus far received far too little consideration.*

This is due in part to the mistaken assumption that the relation between initial standing and increment can be adequately handled by relatively simple statistical procedures. This is by no means true. The problem is complicated by sampling factors, † by differential practice effects, by content differences, and by differential reliability at various ages, after varying amounts of test experience, and for different levels of intelligence. Nevertheless it is in our opinion one of the most basic questions in the entire field of mental measurement. The need for instruments of measurement sufficiently refined to measure *increments* of growth over stated periods of time has been made increasingly evident by a number of recent scientific controversies, of which the nature-nurture question is but one example. A scale made up of items selected to yield the maximal correlation between earlier and later testings would at least help to make sure that the functions measured on the two occasions were psychologically similar. In the absence of information on this all-important point it is difficult, if not impossible, to say which of the three factors previously mentioned is chiefly responsible for the comparatively low predictive value of tests given to young children.

* A beginning in this direction has recently been made by M. F. Roff (1941) in "A Statistical Study of the Development of Intelligence Test Performance," *Journal of Psychology*, 11 : 371–86 (1941).

† See the *Thirty-Ninth Yearbook of the National Society for the Study of Education* (*Intelligence: Its Nature and Nurture*) (Bloomington, Illinois: Public School Publishing Company, 1940), Part I, Chapter 12.

VII. CORRELATION BETWEEN THE MINNESOTA PRESCHOOL SCALES AND THE MERRILL-PALMER SCALE

TRANSMUTATION OF SCORES ON THE MERRILL-PALMER SCALE INTO IQ-EQUIVALENTS

In the Manual of Instructions for the Merrill-Palmer scale (Stutsman, 1931, p. 106), its author points out that "it is impracticable to use the intelligence quotient with the Merrill-Palmer test scale. At the different chronological-age levels the range of IQ's at -2.5σ varies from 58 to 70. At -2.0σ it varies from 66 to 79 and at -1.5σ from 74 to 83. . . . At the other end of the distributions the variation is even greater. At $+2.5\sigma$ the IQ varies from 122 to 165; at $+2.0\sigma$ from 119 to 154 and at $+1.5\sigma$ from 114 to 141. It is apparent that with this amount of variation, such an index has little significance."

The reason for these markedly divergent values in an index that many have been accustomed to think of as having a stable meaning, regardless of the age of the child, is the fact that for this test the standard deviations of mental age do not increase in proportion to advancing chronological age— a condition necessary for the valid use of the IQ. Instead they increase at an irregular rate up to the end of the fourth year, after which they decrease. Stutsman therefore recommends that either percentile ranks or standard deviation units be employed as interpretative measures.

Certain objections, however, may be raised to each of these alternatives. As every competent statistician knows, percentile ranks are not suitable measures to be used in computation because of their unequal spacing, which means that the middle values are not comparable with those of the extremes. For comparing the standing of individual children with others of their age the percentile method is valuable because of its directness and simplicity. For research purposes, when individual test results are to receive further statistical treatment, some other method of specifying a child's standing should be employed.

Standard scores, derived by dividing a child's deviation from the mean by the standard deviation of his age group, are not open to this objection since units so obtained are assumed to be equally spaced.* Nevertheless, the fact that the numerical values thus obtained do not correspond to the distribution of IQ's but center around zero as a mean does not make for easy comparison of one with another.

We have accordingly followed essentially the same principle in expressing the results of the Merrill-Palmer scale as we used with the Minnesota scales (see pages 43–45).† That is, we have substituted an IQ-Equivalent of 100 for the mean score at each age as given in Table 27, page 237, of Stutsman's monograph (1931) and have taken 17.5 IQ points as the equivalent of a divergence of one standard deviation above or below the mean, again using the deviations of point score as presented in the table. As was noted before, this procedure differs from the conventional practice of setting the mean at 50 and the standard deviation at 10 only in its use of different constants, designed to make the numerical system correspond more closely to that of the familiar IQ. Again, we have called these values IQ-Equivalents because of the difference in the method of derivation. It should be noted, however, that our method automatically insures that a given IQ-E value will have the same significance at all ages, whereas IQ's derived by the more conventional method will have constant meaning only if certain rigid statistical conditions are maintained. Although it is evident that the values so obtained are subject to whatever systematic errors of calibration may be inherent in the raw scores, the same criticism is applicable to any other interpretative measure based upon those scores. Our procedure at least does away with the gross discrepancies arising when the conventional method of obtaining the IQ is used. It will be noted, however (see Table 15), that the values so obtained, which are derived from Stutsman (1931; Table 27, page 237), appear to have been

* Actually this assumption is not always valid. If the original units from which these deviations are obtained are expressed in terms of a calibrated scale, the assumption holds, but when the original scores are derived from a mere counting of items that may be very unequally spaced for difficulty, the assumption of true equality of the standard scores rests on insecure ground. Yet, even under these conditions the use of standard scores does away with some of the inequality resulting from imperfect scaling, particularly if the irregular spacing does not show a systematic age trend. Purely random errors of calibration tend to be smoothed out by this method.

† A table for transmuting Merrill-Palmer scores into IQ-E's is given in the Appendix.

based upon a far more heterogeneous group than ours. The standard deviations obtained for our group are smaller than those to be expected from truly comparable groups.

Table 15 shows the means and standard deviations of Merrill-Palmer IQ-E's thus obtained in relation to age and sex. Table 16 shows the relationship of Merrill-Palmer IQ-E's to paternal occupation. At each of the three ages considered, the mean IQ-E's run significantly above 100. At all ages the mean IQ-E of the boys is slightly lower than that of the girls.

It was at first thought that the highly selected character of the group given the Merrill-Palmer test provided an adequate explanation for the high mean standing of our cases. The data presented in Table 16, however, indicate that the selective factor is at least not the same as the factor that seemed to operate for the children given tests on the Minnesota scales. In the latter instance a clear relationship appeared between a child's IQ-E and paternal occupation (see Table 6). On the Merrill-Palmer tests no reliable evidence of such relationship appears.

Relationship between IQ-E's on the Minnesota and Merrill-Palmer Scales

Table 17 shows the correlations between IQ-E's on the Minnesota scales and those on the Merrill-Palmer scale when the two measures were given at approximately the same chronological age. No account has been taken of the order in which the tests were given, inasmuch as separate computation with reference to serial order showed no consistent trend in the extent of relationship found. The results shown in Table 17 are very consistent. With but a single exception, the Minnesota nonverbal scale shows a higher correlation with the Merrill-Palmer scale than does the Minnesota verbal scale. For both sexes, for the total group at the two younger age levels, and for the boys in the oldest group, the nonverbal scale alone yields a higher correlation with the Merrill-Palmer than does the total scale. In part this may be ascribed to the fact that neither the Merrill-Palmer nor the Minnesota nonverbal scale makes much demand upon language facility.*

---

* The Merrill-Palmer scale does contain a number of linguistic items, such as the action-agent test, repeating sentences, answering simple questions, and the like, that together make up fifteen of the ninety-three items in the scale. Both scales make some demand on language comprehension, since instructions are given verbally.

TABLE 15.—MEANS AND STANDARD DEVIATIONS OF MERRILL-PALMER IQ-E'S
BY AGE AND SEX

Age in Months	Boys			Girls			Total		
	N	Mean	SD	N	Mean	SD	N	Mean	SD
Under 36 mos.. .	50	107.0	8.6	55	110.1	10.9	105	108.6	9.8
36–47 mos. . . .	93	107.7	8.7	101	114.8	9.9	194	111.4	9.9
Over 47 mos. . .	131	109.0	7.3	134	111.0	8.0	265	110.0	7.7

TABLE 16.—MEAN MERRILL-PALMER IQ-E'S EARNED BY CHILDREN OF DIFFERENT
AGES AND OCCUPATIONAL GROUPS (SEXES COMBINED)

Age in Months	Occupational Group									
	I		II		III		IV		V–VI	
	N	Mean	N	Mean	N	Mean	N	Mean	N	Mean
Under 36 mos. . . .	38	109.9	18	110.8	24	105.6	14	108.9	11	111.1
36–47 mos.	79	114.8	30	111.7	45	109.5	23	106.0	17	108.1
Over 47 mos. . . .	92	111.2	49	109.3	68	108.6	29	109.6	27	110.1

TABLE 17.—CORRELATIONS BETWEEN MINNESOTA AND MERRILL-PALMER IQ-E'S
WHEN BOTH SCALES WERE GIVEN AT APPROXIMATELY THE SAME AGES

Age in Months	Boys			Girls			Total		
	N	r	PE	N	r	PE	N	r	PE
	VERBAL SCALE								
Under 36 . . .	38	.35	.09	51	.39	.08	89	.28	.07
36–47.	81	.28	.07	92	.16	.07	173	.23	.05
Over 47. . . .	121	.16	.06	119	.28	.06	240	.23	.04
	NONVERBAL SCALE								
Under 36 . . .	28	.52	.09	30	.53	.09	58	.52	.06
36–47.	81	.47	.06	92	.31	.06	173	.41	.04
Over 47. . . .	121	.34	.05	119	.26	.06	240	.33	.04
	TOTAL SCALE								
Under 36 . . .	38	.55	.07	51	.29	.09	89	.39	.06
36–47.	81	.38	.06	92	.22	.07	173	.31	.05
Over 47. . . .	121	.25	.06	119	.28	.06	240	.28	.04

Nevertheless the actual items included in the scales duplicate each other in only a few instances and even these items are not scored in the same manner. It is doubtful whether similarity of test content is the sole explanation for the difference in relationships.

Table 18 shows the correlations between the Merrill-Palmer and the Minnesota scales for tests given at different ages and separated by varying intervals of time. Here the sequence of testing is taken into account. The first group of correlations shows the results when the Minnesota test was given first, followed by the Merrill-Palmer after an interval of from six months to two or more years; the second group of correlations shows the results when the order of giving the two tests was reversed. Examination of this table reveals a number of interesting findings. First, there is a definite tendency for the IQ-E's of the girls to maintain greater stability upon retest after a period of time than those of the boys. Of

TABLE 18.—CORRELATIONS BETWEEN MINNESOTA AND MERRILL-PALMER IQ-E'S WHEN TESTS WERE GIVEN AT DIFFERENT AGES AND AFTER VARYING INTERVALS OF TIME

Age in Months		Minnesota Given First						Merrill-Palmer Given First					
At Initial Test	At Retest	Boys		Girls		Total		Boys		Girls		Total	
		N	r	N	r	N	r	N	r	N	r	N	r
		VERBAL SCALE											
Under 36	36–47 . .	34	.12	43	.22	77	.21	30	.32	39	.14	69	.19
Under 36	over 47 . .	36	.15	45	.66	81	.22	31	.15	30	.26	61	.20
36–47	over 47 . .	76	.09	83	.21	159	.16	68	.24	66	.21	134	.27
		NONVERBAL SCALE											
Under 36	36–47 . .	20	.45	18	.36	38	.46		.30	39	.41	69	.40
Under 36	over 47 . .	23	.13	23	.30	46	.28	31	.22	30	.43	61	.27
36–47	over 47 . .	76	.20	83	.30	159	.26	68	.34	66	.20	134	.35
		TOTAL SCALE											
Under 36	36–47 . .	34	.25	43	.28	77	.29	30	.28	39	.25	69	.27
Under 36	over 47 . .	36	.16	45	.50	81	.22	31	.17	30	.38	61	.28
36–47	over 47 . .	76	.12	83	.25	159	.22	68	.31	66	.21	134	.27

the eighteen sex comparisons available from this table, twelve favor the girls. Similar findings for retests on the Minnesota Preschool Scales were reported in the preceding chapter. The explanation probably lies in the greater maturity and consequently greater docility of girls, even at these tender ages (Goodenough, 1928, 1929, 1931; Rust, 1931; and Reynolds, 1928), particularly of those in the upper socio-economic classes, from which, as was previously stated, the majority of our cases were drawn.

The usual finding that correlations between tests increase with age at time of testing and decrease with increasing length of interval between tests does not appear in the case of the Merrill-Palmer test. It has been our experience that this test is not well suited for use with bright children over the age of 48 months because of the small number of items that are sufficiently difficult to offer any real challenge to their ability. As the ceiling of any test is approached, the usefulness of that test definitely decreases.

Finally, we again find evidence of the apparent superiority of the Minnesota nonverbal scale over the verbal scale. Comparison of the data in Table 18 shows that for corresponding age and sex groups there is a higher correlation between the Merrill-Palmer and Minnesota nonverbal IQ-E's than between the Merrill-Palmer and Minnesota verbal IQ-E's in fourteen out of eighteen instances. However, the greater similarity of test content also needs to be considered. This point will be discussed further in Chapter X.

SUMMARY

We have devised a method of transmuting the normative standards given by Stutsman (1931) for the Merrill-Palmer scale into values that have equal significance at the different ages. When the transmuted IQ-E's are compared with those obtained from the Minnesota scale, a positive relationship between results obtained by the two measures is apparent at all ages.

Particularly when the tests are separated by an interval of time, the girls show a reliable tendency toward greater stability of performance than do the boys. Although it is possible that the sex difference represents an earlier stabilization of mental level in females than in males, it is probably more reasonable to assume that better cooperation and greater docility in the test situation—characteristics in which a number of previous investigations have shown that girls are likely to exceed boys—provide sufficient explanation for the difference found. Nevertheless the other possibility is by no means excluded. Because of the theoretical significance of the problem further investigation is desirable.

Regardless of the age of the subjects or the length of the interval between testings, the correlation between the Minnesota nonverbal scale and the Merrill-Palmer scale is significantly higher than that between the Merrill-Palmer and the verbal scale. Although the explanation undoubtedly lies to some extent in the greater similarity of content, the evidence presented elsewhere in this monograph strongly suggests that actual superiority of the nonverbal over the verbal scale has played a part in bringing about these results.

VIII. PREDICTION OF STANDING ON THE 1916 STANFORD-BINET FROM THE MINNESOTA PRESCHOOL SCALES

NATURE OF THE DATA

It has been our practice to have children brought to the institute for annual testing at a date corresponding as closely as possible to the midpoint between birthdays. For various reasons it has not always been feasible to adhere to this rule as closely for children of preschool age as for older children, a fact that accounts for the less rigidly controlled age groupings used in reporting findings on the preschool tests.

The Stanford-Binet test (1916 revision) was given at annual intervals to children who had previously been enrolled in the institute's nursery school, as well as to a fairly large group of outside cases, up to the time when the 1937 revision became available. Thereafter this new form was substituted. Results from the 1937 revision will be reported in a following chapter.

With the majority of children the Binet tests were not used until the age of 5 1/2 years. A small number, however, were given this test at 4 1/2. In some instances the earlier administration of the Binet was resorted to because of exceptionally high standing on the Minnesota test, leading us to feel that the child had not been adequately measured because he approached too closely the ceiling of the preschool test. Although the number of these cases is not large and the majority of the children were examined as a matter of general rather than specific interest, the composition of the group given the Stanford-Binet at the age of 4 1/2 is not entirely comparable to that of the groups tested at later ages. From the age of 5 1/2 on, the Stanford-Binet was made a routine part of the testing program.

CORRELATION BETWEEN STANDING ON THE MINNESOTA PRESCHOOL SCALES AND LATER STANDING ON THE 1916 STANFORD-BINET

Table 19 shows the correlations between IQ-E's on the Minnesota scales earned by children under the age of 36 months and their IQ's on the Stanford-Binet at various suc-

ceeding ages. The sexes are considered both separately and to-
gether. Table 20 presents the figures for the group given the
Minnesota test between the ages of 36 and 47 months and
Table 21 those for the group first tested at 48 months or older.

The tendency for the early IQ-E's of girls to show slightly
higher predictive value than those of boys, suggested by the
results of the Minnesota and the Merrill-Palmer tests, is not
entirely corroborated by these findings. For the two younger

TABLE 19.—CORRELATIONS BETWEEN IQ-E'S ON THE MINNESOTA SCALES EARNED
BY CHILDREN UNDER 36 MONTHS AND THEIR SUBSEQUENT IQ'S ON THE
1916 STANFORD-BINET

Age in Years at Taking S-B	Boys			Girls			Total Group		
	N	r	SD Minn. S-B	N	r	SD Minn. S-B	N	r	SD Minn. S-B
VERBAL SCALE									
4 1/2*	...	...	... ...	...	...	... ...	31	.75	13.6 12.1
5 1/2	29	.10	11.6 14.1	23	.24	13.2 13.5	52	.16	12.5 13.8
6 1/2	29	.14	9.0 10.5	28	.41	16.0 14.4	57	.33	14.2 12.6
7 1/2	28	.30	9.8 10.9	37	.41	11.0 12.5	65	.37	10.5 11.9
8 1/2*	...	...	... ...	...	...	... ...	47	.42	13.4 14.7
9 1/2*	...	...	... ...	...	...	... ...	28	.22	12.1 15.1
TOTAL SCALE									
4 1/2*	...	...	... ...	...	...	... ...	31	.75	11.9 12.1
5 1/2	29	.18	10.9 14.1	23	.37	11.0 13.5	52	.25	11.2 13.8
6 1/2	29	.15	7.5 10.5	28	.51	16.0 14.4	57	.40	12.5 12.6
7 1/2	28	.32	9.3 10.9	37	.56	10.7 12.5	65	.48	10.3 11.9
8 1/2*	...	...	... ...	...	...	... ...	47	.45	12.6 14.7
9 1/2*	...	...	... ...	...	...	... ...	28	.30	10.8 15.1

* The number of cases at these ages did not warrant separation of the sexes.

age groups the same trend appears, but for the oldest group,
which includes children first tested at 48 months and over,
the tendency is in the opposite direction. It appears likely,
therefore, that if a sex difference exists at all it is of a relatively transitory character.

A comparison of the predictive value of the verbal and the
nonverbal scales reveals much the same general trend as was
pointed out in the two earlier sections. In spite of its slightly
lower reliability as indicated by the correlations between
Form A and Form B for the standardization group and in
spite of its smaller number of items, the nonverbal scale predicts later standing on the Stanford-Binet somewhat better
than does the verbal scale for the younger group of subjects.

TABLE 20.—CORRELATIONS BETWEEN IQ-E's ON THE MINNESOTA SCALES EARNED BY CHILDREN OF 36-47 MONTHS AND THEIR SUBSEQUENT IQ's ON THE 1916 STANFORD-BINET

Age in Years at Taking S-B	Boys				Girls				Total Group			
	N	r	SD Minn.	SD S-B	N	r	SD Minn.	SD S-B	N	r	SD Minn.	SD S-B
VERBAL SCALE												
4 1/2 . . .	24	.43	9.7	12.5	30	.56	9.5	12.6	54	.51	9.6	12.6
5 1/2 . . .	44	.59	10.5	15.7	39	.53	10.0	12.8	83	.71	10.7	14.6
6 1/2 . . .	35	.45	10.6	11.7	32	.56	11.0	14.5	67	.51	11.1	13.1
7 1/2 . . .	36	.30	9.9	10.6	37	.53	10.5	14.1	73	.44	10.1	12.0
8 1/2 . . .	33	.51	10.8	11.0	26	.62	10.3	18.8	59	.55	11.0	15.0
9 1/2*	...	...	...	...	...	...	...	...	41	.48	10.8	19.5
10 1/2*	...	...	...	...	...	...	...	...	32	.54	12.5	18.0
NONVERBAL SCALE												
4 1/2 . . .	24	.58	10.8	12.5	30	.51	12.4	12.6	54	.54	11.6	12.6
5 1/2 . . .	44	.60	14.6	15.7	39	.63	13.3	12.8	83	.62	14.2	14.6
6 1/2 . . .	35	.30	11.5	11.7	32	.57	12.0	14.5	67	.45	12.0	13.1
7 1/2 . . .	36	.48	12.3	10.6	37	.63	13.8	14.1	73	.56	13.3	12.0
8 1/2 . . .	33	.64	14.0	11.0	26	.54	14.0	18.8	59	.57	14.2	15.0
9 1/2*	...	...	...	...	...	...	...	...	41	.73	14.1	19.5
10 1/2*	...	...	...	...	...	...	...	...	32	.78	15.7	18.0
TOTAL SCALE												
4 1/2 . . .	24	.48	10.1	12.5	30	.55	10.6	12.6	54	.52	10.5	12.6
5 1/2 . . .	44	.68	11.7	15.7	39	.60	11.3	12.8	83	.66	11.9	14.6
6 1/2 . . .	35	.41	10.2	11.7	32	.67	11.3	14.5	67	.55	11.1	13.1
7 1/2 . . .	36	.37	9.3	10.6	37	.71	10.9	14.1	73	.57	10.4	12.0
8 1/2 . . .	33	.67	11.9	11.0	26	.67	10.9	18.8	59	.64	11.8	15.0
9 1/2*	...	...	...	...	...	...	...	...	41	.65	11.7	19.5
10 1/2*	...	...	...	...	...	...	...	...	32	.73	13.9	18.0

* The number of cases at these ages did not warrant separation of the sexes.

For the oldest group the difference is less clear cut, a fact that may be due, at least in part, to the relatively small number of nonverbal items sufficiently difficult to challenge the ability of the older and brighter children in our group. A glance at the table of norms given in the Manual of Directions will show that the ceiling of the nonverbal scale is appreciably lower than that of the verbal scale.*

Table 22 shows the median correlation of the IQ-E's on verbal, nonverbal and total scales with later Stanford-Binet IQ's for each of the three age groups. These figures are taken

* The mean nonverbal IQ-E of the oldest group in these comparisons is approximately 110.2. Their mean verbal IQ-E is 112.0. At the age of 54 months thirty-six out of the fifty-five nonverbal items must be passed to attain this level; at the same age the number of items that must be passed to reach the verbal mean is fifty-five out of ninety.

TABLE 21.—CORRELATIONS BETWEEN IQ-E'S ON THE MINNESOTA SCALES EARNED BY CHILDREN OVER 47 MONTHS AND THEIR SUBSEQUENT IQ'S ON THE 1916 STANFORD-BINET

Age in Years at Taking S-B	Boys				Girls				Total Group			
	N	r	SD Minn.	SD S-B	N	r	SD Minn.	SD S-B	N	r	SD Minn.	SD S-B
VERBAL SCALE												
4 1/2	40	.56	11.1	13.7	36	.50	10.6	13.2	76	.53	10.9	13.5
5 1/2	68	.51	12.1	14.9	59	.25	10.1	11.5	127	.42	11.5	13.2
6 1/2	76	.67	11.5	13.9	77	.54	9.6	14.7	153	.59	10.6	14.3
7 1/2	68	.63	11.4	12.9	73	.54	9.9	13.2	141	.59	10.5	13.0
8 1/2	52	.48	10.7	14.2	46	.51	9.6	15.4	98	.49	10.2	14.8
9 1/2	45	.65	11.9	20.0	45	.50	11.4	17.4	90	.58	11.6	18.8
10 1/2	36	.68	11.3	20.0	34	.33	10.6	18.6	70	.52	11.2	19.9
11 1/2*		...	...			...	...		49	.57	11.6	18.2
12 1/2, 13 1/2, 14 1/2*		...	...			...	...		37	.75	8.6	18.8
NONVERBAL SCALE												
4 1/2	40	.59	14.1	13.7	36	.47	12.1	13.2	76	.52	13.3	13.5
5 1/2	68	.42	13.3	14.9	59	.43	12.2	11.5	127	.43	13.1	13.2
6 1/2	76	.56	13.6	13.9	77	.58	13.2	14.7	153	.57	13.5	14.3
7 1/2	68	.68	15.3	12.9	73	.41	10.6	13.2	141	.55	13.1	13.0
8 1/2	52	.54	13.8	14.2	46	.31	11.1	15.4	98	.43	12.6	14.8
9 1/2	45	.65	10.8	20.0	45	.50	12.8	17.4	90	.56	11.9	18.8
10 1/2	36	.65	15.0	20.0	34	.28	12.7	18.6	70	.49	13.9	19.9
11 1/2*		...	...			...	...		49	.66	13.0	18.2
12 1/2, 13 1/2, 14 1/2*		...	...			...	...		37	.51	16.1	18.8
TOTAL SCALE												
4 1/2	40	.68	11.8	13.7	36	.54	11.4	13.2	76	.61	11.7	13.5
5 1/2	68	.53	11.9	14.9	59	.38	11.2	11.5	127	.48	11.8	13.2
6 1/2	76	.72	11.3	13.9	77	.59	10.5	14.7	153	.65	10.9	14.3
7 1/2	68	.74	12.1	12.9	73	.56	9.5	13.2	141	.65	10.9	13.0
8 1/2	52	.61	10.6	14.2	46	.50	10.4	15.4	98	.55	10.5	14.8
9 1/2	45	.73	12.1	20.0	45	.57	11.7	17.4	90	.65	11.9	18.8
10 1/2	36	.76	12.4	20.0	34	.35	11.1	18.6	70	.58	11.8	19.9
11 1/2*		...	...			...	...		49	.70	12.7	18.2
12 1/2, 13 1/2, 14 1/2*		...	...			...	...		37	.73	10.4	18.8

* The number of cases at these ages did not warrant separation of the sexes.

TABLE 22.—MEDIAN CORRELATIONS BETWEEN MINNESOTA IQ-E'S AT DIFFERENT AGES AND STANFORD-BINET IQ'S AT AGES RANGING FROM 4 1/2 TO 13 1/2 YEARS*

Age in Months at Taking Minnesota	Median Correlations with Stanford-Binet			Median SD of Stanford-Binet IQ
	Verbal Scale	Nonverbal Scale	Total Scale	
Under 36.	+.37	...	+.45	11.9
36–47	+.51	+.57	+.64	15.0
48 and over	+.57	+.52	+.65	13.0

* Summarized from Tables 19–21.

74

from Tables 19–21. The tendency for the correlations to increase with advancing age of the child at time of first testing is very apparent in both the verbal scale and the total scale. The drop in the median correlation for children past the age of 4 years in the case of the nonverbal scale, as was pointed out before, is probably due to its less complete adequacy for measuring the older and brighter children in this particular age group.

Inspection of Tables 19–21 reveals a marked difference between the correlational trend for the Minnesota scales and those from other studies in which children have been tested at regular intervals of time. Practically all studies in which the ages of the children and the intervals between testings have been simultaneously controlled have shown a regular tendency toward decrease in correlation as the interval between testings is increased. No such trend appears in our data. There is a distinct relationship between magnitude of correlation and age of child at first testing, but as far as can be judged from this study the Minnesota test predicts standing on the Stanford-Binet quite as accurately over an interval of six or seven years as over an interval of one or two years. Just why this exception to so general a rule should occur is uncertain. It may result from the method of scale calibration employed or it may be a function of the selection of test items. One would perhaps like to think that the test is not highly affected by the changes in experience and training that affect the various members of a group in a differential fashion and therefore bring about an increasing number of changes in relative position with the passage of time. However, we are at a loss to say why this should be more true of the Minnesota scales than of other tests.

DISCUSSION

In accordance with the findings of other investigators using different tests, our results show only a rather low relationship between the mental standing of children under the age of 3 years as indicated by the Minnesota Preschool Scales and their performance on the Stanford-Binet after an interval of several years. For children who were beyond the age of 3 at the time of first testing, the prediction of later standing is more dependable.

As a matter of fact, when the correlations presented in Table 22 are compared with those reported by Terman in 1919* on retests by the Stanford-Binet after intervals varying from one day to seven years, the difference is decidedly less marked than it at first appears. The correlation reported by Terman for 428 retests of 315 cases of heterogeneity indicated by an *SD* of 21.8 points of Stanford-Binet IQ is +.93. Because our group is far more homogeneous in ability, a correction for range is necessary. † When this correction is applied, utilizing for this purpose the median *SD*'s of Stanford-Binet IQ shown in Table 22,‡ the correlations are materially increased. The corrected values are shown in Table 23.

TABLE 23.—MEDIAN CORRECTED CORRELATIONS BETWEEN MINNESOTA IQ-E's AT
DIFFERENT AGES AND STANFORD-BINET IQ's AT AGES RANGING FROM
4 1/2 TO 13 1/2 YEARS*

Age in Months at Taking Minnesota	Median Corrected Correlations with Stanford-Binet		
	Verbal Scale	Nonverbal Scale	Total Scale
Under 36	+.56	. . .	+.61
36–47	+.65	+.71	+.77
48 and over	+.76	+.71	+.82

* Corrected to correspond to IQ variability equal to that of the retest group reported by Terman (1919) for whom the *SD* was 21.8 IQ points.

The children retested in Terman's study obviously make up a far more heterogeneous group than is likely to be found in any single school or classroom. We have chosen this report for comparison with our data because its results seem to be most frequently quoted for the correlation between test and retest on the 1916 Stanford-Binet. Moreover, except in those instances where special investigations of retest correlation have been set up, the cases available for study are always likely to include a disproportionate number at the extremes of the distribution. This of course results in high standard deviations. The reason is fairly obvious. In the course of routine testing in the psychological or educational clinic, children decidedly above or below average in intelligence are encoun-

* L. M. Terman, *The Intelligence of School Children* (Boston: Houghton Mifflin Company, 1919), pp. 138–44.
† See T. L. Kelley, *Statistical Method* (New York: Macmillan, 1923), pp. 223–25.
‡ We have made this correction in terms of Stanford-Binet variability rather than that shown on the Minnesota scales in order that the results may be compared directly with that reported by Terman.

tered much more often than their frequency in the school population would lead one to expect. Questions of extra promotion or of transfer to a special class, as well as disciplinary problems arising from unsuitability of classroom requirements to the child's mental level, bring the intellectual deviates to the mental examiner in disproportionately large numbers. And since most of the reported data on retests after a period of time have been based on cases tested for practical service to the school and to the child, rather than for purposes of research, it seems likely that the majority of these reports have likewise included a wider range of talent than would be found for groups more nearly typical of the general population.

Data entirely comparable to ours are hard to find in the literature. Bayley (1940) reports correlations between the California Preschool Scale given at semiannual intervals from 2 to 5 years and the 1916 Stanford-Binet given at ages 6 and 7. Her results follow the usual pattern of increase with increasing age of child at first testing and decrease with increasing intervals between tests. The group is somewhat more heterogeneous than ours (*SD* of Stanford-Binet IQ is between 15 and 16 IQ points). The correlations for the 2-year-olds range from +.52 to +.59, those for the 3-year-olds from +.58 to +.70, and those for the 4-year-olds from +.60 to +.77. For somewhat older children (ages 5–9) and for shorter intervals between testings Ebert (1941) reports slightly higher correlations for retests on the 1916 Stanford-Binet. Her figures run from +.56 to +.76 for groups with *SD*'s ranging from 10 to 14 IQ points.

It will be noted that there is a sharp reduction in the number of cases given the 1916 Stanford-Binet after the age of 9 1/2 years. This is due to our change to the 1937 revision of the Stanford-Binet, which by special arrangement with the authors was made in the fall of 1936. Results obtained with the use of the revised form are reported in the following chapter.

IX. PREDICTION OF STANDING ON THE 1937 STANFORD-BINET FROM THE MINNESOTA PRESCHOOL SCALES

1916 AND 1937 REVISIONS OF THE STANFORD-BINET COMPARED

To date few comparisons of the correlations between the 1916 and 1937 revisions of the Stanford-Binet and other measures of intelligence have appeared in the literature. Terman and Merrill (1937) report correlations ranging from +.85 to +.90 for various age groups. Traxler (1941) reports a somewhat closer agreement between the IQ's earned on the fifth revision of the Kuhlmann-Anderson group test and the 1937 revision than was found for the 1916 revision. A similar difference in favor of the 1937 revision appeared when the fourth edition of the Kuhlmann-Anderson test was used. However, the differences are small, the sampling of subjects is not the same, and there is some reason to think that the mean interval between the administration of the individual test and the group test may have been greater in the case of the 1916 revision than in that of the 1937 revision.* The correlations between the 1916 Stanford-Binet and the fourth and fifth editions of the Kuhlmann-Anderson were +.55 and +.60 respectively; for the 1937 revision the corresponding figures are +.62 and +.65.

Ebert (1941) in a well-controlled comparison of the two scales, in which children between the ages of 5 and 10 years were used as subjects, shows that, although there is little consistent change in the mean IQ's obtained by the 1916 revision within the age range covered by the study, the IQ's for the 1937 revision show a marked tendency to increase after the age of 8 years. This tendency is accompanied by a significant increase in variability.† At all ages the variability of the 1937 revision is greater than that of the 1916 revision. Correlations between the 1916 and the 1937 revisions tend to be slightly

---

* The fourth edition of the Kuhlmann-Anderson test was used from 1937 to 1939, the fifth edition in 1940. The 1937 revision of the Stanford-Binet obviously could not have been administered at an earlier date than that of its publication, but it is probable that many of the tests by the 1916 revision were given some time previous to 1937, inasmuch as the Binet testing was not done specifically for the purposes of this investigation.

† See article by Goodenough cited in note, page 44.

higher than those found for retests by the 1916 revision and, unlike the latter, show little consistent tendency to decrease with increasing intervals between testings. Retests by the 1937 revision cover only a two-year span and include no tests of 5-year-olds. The results are accordingly not entirely comparable to those from retests by the 1916 revision, but for similar ages and intervals the correlations run slightly higher than those based upon the earlier form.

FINDINGS OF THE PRESENT STUDY

The number of our cases given the 1937 revision of the Stanford is unfortunately too small to warrant handling the data for Form L and Form M separately. Only a small num-

TABLE 24.—CORRELATIONS BETWEEN IQ-E'S ON THE MINNESOTA SCALES EARNED BY CHILDREN UNDER 36 MONTHS AND THEIR SUBSEQUENT IQ'S ON THE 1937 STANFORD-BINET*

Age in Years at Taking S-B	N	Verbal Scale			Total Scale		
		r	SD		r	SD	
			Minn.	S-B		Minn.	S-B
7 1/2	26	+.31	10.0	19.7	+.26	10.2	19.7
8 1/2	24	+.08	10.8	22.1	+.22	12.2	22.1
9 1/2	21	−.11	10.2	17.9	+.15	9.1	17.9
10 1/2	27	+.01	9.8	16.2	+.19	9.0	16.2
11 1/2	22	+.26	13.2	17.3	+.45	11.0	17.3
12 1/2	21	+.17	11.9	20.3	+.18	11.4	20.3

* The number of subjects in this age group given the new Stanford-Binet before the age of 7 1/2 was too few to warrant the reporting of correlations. The minimal interval between test and retest is therefore at least four years.

ber of the children included in the growth study have been given more than two testings with the 1937 scale. The two forms were used in alternate years in order to lessen the effect of practice, Form L always being given first with a change to Form M the following year. Inasmuch as Terman and Merrill (1937) have reported a median correlation between Form L and Form M of +.91, which is about as high as most investigators have found for retests on the same scale, and since the means and standard deviations of the two forms are very similar at all ages, the amount of error introduced by combining results for the two forms is presumably not great. Because of the relatively small number of cases tested at each age we have made no attempt at sex comparisons.

TABLE 25.—CORRELATIONS BETWEEN IQ-E's ON THE MINNESOTA SCALES EARNED BY CHILDREN BETWEEN 36 AND 47 MONTHS AND THEIR SUBSEQUENT IQ's ON THE 1937 STANFORD-BINET

Age in Years at Taking S-B	N	Verbal Scale			Nonverbal Scale			Total Scale		
		r	SD Minn.	SD S-B	r	SD Minn.	SD S-B	r	SD Minn.	SD S-B
4 1/2 . .	29	+.71	11.7	14.8	+.67	12.1	14.8	+.69	12.2	14.8
5 1/2 . .	29	+.47	8.2	13.3	+.72	9.4	13.3	+.66	8.0	13.3
6 1/2 . .	37	+.72	10.1	15.4	+.63	10.2	15.4	+.76	10.0	15.4
7 1/2 . .	31	+.55	10.5	16.3	+.50	11.2	16.3	+.56	10.9	16.3
8 1/2 . .	28	+.38	10.8	21.2	+.41	11.5	21.2	+.42	11.2	21.2
9 1/2 . .	31	+.31	9.2	17.4	+.36	11.9	17.4	+.31	10.0	17.4
10 1/2 .	28	+.25	10.0	16.6	+.48	12.4	16.6	+.40	8.9	16.6
11 1/2 .	22	+.36	11.9	19.5	+.74	17.1	19.5	+.66	13.5	19.5
12 1/2 .	28	+.43	11.3	*18.3	+.65	15.9	18.3	+.61	13.1	18.3

TABLE 26.—CORRELATIONS BETWEEN IQ-E's ON THE MINNESOTA SCALES EARNED BY CHILDREN 48 MONTHS AND OVER AND THEIR SUBSEQUENT IQ's ON THE 1937 STANFORD-BINET

Age in Years at Taking S-B	N	Verbal Scale			Nonverbal Scale			Total Scale		
		r	SD Minn.	SD S-B	r	SD Minn.	SD S-B	r	SD Minn.	SD S-B
4 1/2 . .	29	+.75	11.6	15.5	+.66	15.5	15.5	+.76	13.3	15.5
5 1/2 . .	50	+.57	11.4	14.3	+.71	14.0	14.3	+.69	12.7	14.3
6 1/2 . .	55	+.55	10.7	16.0	+.44	13.1	16.0	+.58	11.7	16.0
7 1/2 . .	64	+.63	11.1	17.5	+.67	12.3	17.5	+.68	11.6	17.5
8 1/2 . .	58	+.63	9.9	19.9	+.68	13.8	19.9	+.72	11.0	19.9
9 1/2 . .	48	+.54	10.7	18.0	+.54	12.3	18.0	+.57	10.3	18.0
10 1/2 .	47	+.60	9.8	18.8	+.60	11.9	18.8	+.70	10.5	18.8
11 1/2 .	43	+.61	11.3	19.0	+.63	13.6	19.0	+.73	11.2	19.0
12 1/2 .	45	+.37	9.9	16.6	+.43	10.7	16.6	+.43	9.9	16.6
13 1/2 .	43	+.34	9.5	15.2	+.45	14.1	15.2	+.50	10.3	15.2
14 1/2 .	27	+.50	7.7	17.6	+.51	15.3	17.6	+.62	9.0	17.6

TABLE 27.—MEDIAN CORRELATIONS BETWEEN IQ-E's ON THE MINNESOTA SCALES EARNED BY CHILDREN OF VARIOUS AGES AND THEIR SUBSEQUENT IQ's ON THE 1916 AND 1937 STANFORD-BINETS

Age in Months at Taking Minnesota	Median Correlations with Stanford-Binet					
	Verbal Scale		Nonverbal Scale		Total Scale	
	1916	1937	1916	1937	1916	1937
Under 36	+.37	+.13	+.37	...	+.45	+.21
36–47	+.51	+.43	+.60	+.63	+.61	+.61
48 and over . .	+.57	+.57	+.52	+.60	+.65	+.68

Table 24 shows the correlations between the Minnesota IQ-E's and the 1937 Stanford IQ's for children first tested before the age of 36 months. Tables 25 and 26 show the corresponding figures for the two older groups. Comparison of Tables 24–26 with the corresponding tables based upon the 1916 Stanford-Binet and presented in Chapter VIII shows no consistent difference in the relation of the Minnesota scales to the two revisions of the Binet. Of the eight medians compared in Table 27 the correlation with the 1916 revision is slightly higher in three instances; the 1937 revision gives a higher correlation in three cases; and the two are equal in two instances. None of the differences is high enough to be significant.

The apparent superiority of the nonverbal over the verbal scale is again shown in these figures. The difference, though not great, is fairly consistent. Of the twenty comparisons afforded by Tables 25 and 26, the nonverbal scale leads in thirteen instances, the verbal in five instances, and in the remaining two instances the correlations are equal. In the only four instances in which the differences between the correlations approach statistical significance (Table 25, ages 5 1/2, 10 1/2, 11 1/2, 12 1/2) the advantage in each case lies with the nonverbal scale. The fact that the nonverbal scale does not show quite such an advantage for the oldest group of children as it does for the middle group is, as was pointed out before, probably due to its lower ceiling. It is to be regretted that a larger number of difficult nonverbal items was not included.

X. PREDICTION OF STANDING ON THE ARTHUR SCALE, FORM I, FROM THE MINNESOTA PRESCHOOL SCALES

RELIABILITY OF THE ARTHUR SCALE

The scale of performance, or nonlanguage, tests devised by Dr. Grace Arthur (1930, 1933) is widely used in clinical testing. Because it is an individual test that makes no demand upon language usage and involves only a minimal degree of language comprehension, the scale has been found particularly valuable for use with children whose knowledge of English is limited and with those suffering from marked defects of speech or hearing. As a matter of fact, although the instructions are usually given verbally, if necessary they can be communicated for the most part by pantomime.

Although two forms of the scale are available, Arthur notes in Volume I of her Manual (1930) that Form I is distinctly more dependable than Form II. The use of Form II is not recommended except in special cases, such as instances of special coaching on Form I, or when a check test is desired. Our data are based entirely upon Form I; we have not used Form II at any time.

In Volume II of her Manual (1933) Arthur presents scattergrams showing the relationship between Form I and Form II of her scale and between the results of Form I and those of the 1916 Stanford-Binet or the 1922 Kuhlmann-Binet.* As this constitutes the best evidence available on the reliability and validity of the Arthur scale for comparatively unselected groups, we have worked out the correlations indicated by the scattergrams. The results are shown in Tables 28 and 29.

The striking thing about Table 28 is the sudden and marked increase in the standard deviations of IQ's after the age of 11 years. This renders the self-correlations at these ages quite incomparable to those obtained earlier. We have not attempted to make a statistical correction for the difference because of the uncertainty as to its cause. It may be either a function of the scale itself or the result of some special selective factor influencing the samplings of subjects at the

---

* In these correlations IQ's from the 1916 Stanford-Binet and the 1922 Kuhlmann-Binet are used interchangeably.

TABLE 28.—CORRELATIONS BETWEEN IQ'S ON FORM I AND FORM II OF THE ARTHUR SCALE AT VARIOUS AGES

Age in Years	N	r	PE_r	SD_1	SD_1,1
6.	41	.53	.08	13.5	13.5
7.	52	.59	.06	13.0	15.0
8.	53	.53	.07	12.1	12.0
9.	49	.67	.05	9.5	14.3
10	51	.56	.06	12.6	14.3
11*.	54	.38	.08	21.2	22.2
12*.	50	.63	.06	16.0	20.7
13*.	49	.66	.05	20.6	21.6
14*.	51	.60	.06	15.6	19.2

* The correlations at these ages are not directly comparable with those in the first part of the table because of the great increase in variability of the groups from which the r's have been computed.

TABLE 29.—CORRELATIONS BETWEEN ARTHUR IQ'S AND BINET IQ'S* AT VARIOUS AGES†

Age in Years	N	r	PE_r	SD Arthur	SD Binet
6.	54	.76	.04	13.4	10.3
7.	50	.61	.06	11.9	11.5
8.	44	.74	.05	16.9	12.8
9.	41	.81	.04	14.1	10.5
10	40	.54	.08	17.0	12.2

* The Binet IQ's are in part 1916 Stanford-Binet and in part 1922 Kuhlmann-Binet. Arthur does not present results for the two separately.
† These correlations are computed from the scattergrams on pages 55–59 of Arthur's Manual, Volume 2.

later ages. There seems to be no doubt, however, that if the variability were reduced to the level shown for ages 6–10, the magnitude of the later r's would be materially reduced. Our own experience in using the scale with older children leads us to question its usefulness, except with the mentally retarded, after the age of 10 or 11 years. Save for a few exceptional cases, we have therefore discontinued its use after the age of 10 1/2.

FINDINGS OF THE PRESENT STUDY

Tables 30, 31, and 32 show the correlations between the Minnesota scales and the Arthur scale administered two or more years subsequently. As was previously reported for the Merrill-Palmer scale (which also makes little demand upon

TABLE 30.—CORRELATIONS BETWEEN IQ-E'S ON THE MINNESOTA SCALES EARNED BY CHILDREN UNDER 36 MONTHS AND THEIR SUBSEQUENT IQ'S ON THE ARTHUR SCALE

Minn. IQ-E	Arthur IQ at Age (in Years)				
	N	r	PE_r	SD	
				Minn.	Arthur
VERBAL SCALE					
5 1/2 68	+.12	.08		12.2	10.3
6 1/2 66	+.17	.08		11.2	12.9
7 1/2 63	+.21	.08		11.7	14.1
8 1/2 49	+.25	.08		11.7	17.5
9 1/2 33	+.44	.09		12.5	14.5
TOTAL SCALE					
5 1/2 68	+.24	.07		10.9	10.3
6 1/2 66	+.31	.07		10.8	12.9
7 1/2 63	+.31	.07		10.6	14.1
8 1/2 49	+.36	.09		11.0	17.5
9 1/2 33	+.43	.09		11.2	14.5

TABLE 31.—CORRELATIONS BETWEEN IQ-E'S ON THE MINNESOTA SCALES EARNED BY CHILDREN BETWEEN 36 AND 47 MONTHS AND THEIR SUBSEQUENT IQ'S ON THE ARTHUR SCALE

Minn. IQ-E	Arthur IQ at Age (in Years)				
	N	r	PE_r	SD	
				Minn.	Arthur
VERBAL					
5 1/2 96	+.38	.06		10.8	10.1
6 1/2 95	+.44	.06		11.6	11.6
7 1/2 77	+.34	.07		9.9	13.5
8 1/2 65	+.48	.06		11.3	16.2
9 1/2 52	+.28	.09		11.0	13.5
10 1/2 30	+.37	.11		11.8	10.6
NONVERBAL					
5 1/2 96	+.61	.05		12.9	10.1
6 1/2 95	+.61	.05		11.8	11.6
7 1/2 77	+.59	.05		11.3	13.5
8 1/2 65	+.63	.05		13.3	16.2
9 1/2 52	+.42	.08		10.4	13.5
10 1/2 30	+.39	.10		11.4	10.6
TOTAL					
5 1/2 96	+.52	.05		11.5	10.1
6 1/2 95	+.54	.05		11.5	11.6
7 1/2 77	+.50	.06		9.9	13.5
8 1/2 65	+.60	.05		11.9	16.2
9 1/2 52	+.38	.08		10.3	13.5
10 1/2 30	+.38	.11		11.3	10.6

TABLE 32.—CORRELATIONS BETWEEN IQ-E's ON THE MINNESOTA SCALES EARNED
BY CHILDREN OVER 47 MONTHS AND THEIR SUBSEQUENT ARTHUR IQ's

Minn. IQ-E				Arthur IQ at Age (in Years)	
	N	r	PE_r	SD	
				Minn.	Arthur
VERBAL					
5 1/2 177		+.34	.04	10.5	9.5
6 1/2 164		+.40	.04	10.5	11.4
7 1/2 147		+.31	.05	10.6	13.5
8 1/2 127		+.24	.05	10.4	14.4
9 1/2 99		+.30	.06	11.5	13.0
10 1/2 65		+.31	.07	9.6	11.0
NONVERBAL					
5 1/2 177		+.54	.04	12.3	9.5
6 1/2 164		+.62	.03	12.6	11.4
7 1/2 147		+.45	.04	13.1	13.5
8 1/2 127		+.46	.05	12.5	14.4
9 1/2 99		+.43	.06	11.9	13.0
10 1/2 65		+.45	.07	13.6	11.0
TOTAL					
5 1/2 177		+.48	.04	10.6	9.5
6 1/2 164		+.53	.04	10.8	11.4
7 1/2 147		+.39	.05	11.0	13.5
8 1/2 127		+.38	.05	10.6	14.4
9 1/2 99		+.43	.06	11.5	13.0
10 1/2 65		+.43	.07	10.6	11.0

language), the correlations of our nonverbal scale with the performance scale are consistently higher than are those of the verbal scale. Typically, the correlations for the total scale are intermediate in value between those for the two subscales. The nonverbal score alone predicts later standing on the Arthur better than the combination of the two scales.

SEX DIFFERENCES IN IQ STABILITY

Tables 30–32 present only the values for the sexes combined, but similar tables for boys and girls separately have also been prepared (see Tables 33–35). The results of these comparisons agree with those reported in the preceding chapters. For the youngest age group, in every one of the paired correlations, the relationship is higher for the girls than for the boys. In the middle group the girls lead in twelve out of fifteen instances, the boys in two; in one case the results are equal. For the oldest group the trend is reversed. The figure for the girls exceeds that for the boys in only seven of the eighteen comparisons.

TABLE 33.—CORRELATIONS BETWEEN IQ.E's ON THE MINNESOTA SCALES EARNED BY CHILDREN UNDER 36 MONTHS AND THEIR SUBSEQUENT IQ's ON THE ARTHUR SCALE (SEXES CONSIDERED SEPARATELY)

Age in Years at Taking Arthur	Boys							Girls						
	N	Minnesota		Arthur		r	PEr	N	Minnesota		Arthur		r	PEr
		Mean	SD	Mean	SD				Mean	SD	Mean	SD		
VERBAL SCALE														
5½	35	109.5	12.4	129.7	10.2	.11	.11	33	116.6	10.8	129.7	10.4	.14	.12
6½	31	112.0	11.2	128.8	8.8	−.02	.12	35	118.0	10.5	133.7	15.2	.23	.11
7½	27	110.7	11.0	125.7	10.3	.15	.13	36	115.3	11.9	133.5	15.5	.18	.11
8½	27	111.2	10.9	130.9	17.7	.14	.13	22	115.5	12.1	139.9	15.9	.32	.13
TOTAL SCALE														
5½	35	105.0	10.6	129.7	10.2	.23	.11	33	113.9	9.3	129.7	10.4	.30	.11
6½	31	106.7	9.9	128.8	8.8	.06	.12	35	115.1	10.1	133.7	15.2	.37	.10
7½	27	107.2	9.9	125.7	10.3	.17	.13	36	110.9	10.9	133.5	15.5	.34	.11
8½	27	107.0	10.0	130.9	17.7	.20	.12	22	113.2	11.1	139.9	15.9	.46	.11

TABLE 34.—CORRELATIONS BETWEEN IQ-E's ON THE MINNESOTA SCALES EARNED BY CHILDREN FROM 36 TO 47 MONTHS AND THEIR SUBSEQUENT IQ's ON THE ARTHUR SCALE (SEXES CONSIDERED SEPARATELY)

Age in Years at Taking Arthur	Boys							Girls						
	N	Minnesota Mean	Minnesota SD	Arthur Mean	Arthur SD	r	PE$_r$	N	Minnesota Mean	Minnesota SD	Arthur Mean	Arthur SD	r	PE$_r$
VERBAL SCALE														
5 1/2	46	111.8	10.0	130.2	10.4	.43	.08	50	116.2	11.0	130.5	9.8	.33	.09
6 1/2	44	110.8	11.4	128.7	8.1	.35	.09	51	115.0	11.4	131.9	13.7	.49	.07
7 1/2	31	112.2	8.9	131.1	11.3	−.08	.12	46	114.8	10.5	132.7	14.8	.51	.07
8 1/2	34	108.6	11.0	130.4	14.7	.30	.11	31	117.4	10.5	138.2	16.9	.59	.08
9 1/2	26	109.1	11.3	132.4	13.6	.26	.13	26	115.6	9.5	135.3	13.1	.26	.13
NONVERBAL SCALE														
5 1/2	46	110.9	13.2	130.2	10.4	.59	.06	50	115.7	12.2	130.5	9.8	.63	.06
6 1/2	44	108.5	12.0	128.7	8.1	.54	.07	51	113.9	11.1	131.9	13.7	.68	.05
7 1/2	31	112.7	9.7	131.1	11.3	.20	.11	46	112.5	12.2	132.7	14.8	.75	.04
8 1/2	34	108.1	13.6	130.4	14.7	.59	.08	31	114.0	12.4	138.2	16.9	.63	.07
9 1/2	26	107.9	12.3	132.4	13.6	.35	.12	26	110.8	7.9	135.3	13.1	.54	.10
TOTAL SCALE														
5 1/2	46	112.3	11.2	130.2	10.4	.54	.07	50	116.8	11.4	130.5	9.8	.50	.07
6 1/2	44	110.7	11.3	128.7	8.1	.43	.08	51	115.5	11.1	131.9	13.7	.61	.06
7 1/2	31	113.5	8.9	131.1	11.3	.05	.12	46	114.8	10.5	132.7	14.8	.68	.05
8 1/2	34	109.9	12.2	130.4	14.7	.50	.09	31	115.6	10.9	138.2	16.9	.66	.07
9 1/2	26	109.1	11.0	132.4	13.6	.31	.12	26	114.6	8.8	135.3	13.1	.43	.11

TABLE 35.—CORRELATIONS BETWEEN IQ-E'S ON THE MINNESOTA SCALES EARNED BY CHILDREN OVER 47 MONTHS AND THEIR SUBSEQUENT IQ'S ON THE ARTHUR SCALE (SEXES CONSIDERED SEPARATELY)

Age in Years at Taking Arthur	Boys								Girls							
	N	Minnesota		Arthur		r	PE_r		N	Minnesota		Arthur		r	PE_r
		Mean	SD	Mean	SD					Mean	SD	Mean	SD		
VERBAL SCALE															
5 1/2	84	113.3	10.9	128.6	8.7	.45	.06		93	115.0	10.1	128.1	10.1	.26	.06
6 1/2	81	112.3	11.0	128.7	9.6	.37	.06		83	114.3	9.8	130.5	13.0	.44	.06
7 1/2	68	111.9	10.6	129.6	11.6	.23	.07		79	114.5	10.5	130.6	15.0	.36	.06
8 1/2	67	112.8	11.3	130.0	12.8	.11	.08		60	114.5	9.1	132.8	15.9	.39	.07
9 1/2	51	112.1	12.8	131.5	13.2	.33	.08		48	112.3	10.0	134.3	12.7	.27	.08
10 1/2	37	112.0	10.1	131.9	11.2	.28	.09		28	109.7	8.6	129.8	10.6	.34	.10
NONVERBAL SCALE															
5 1/2	84	112.3	12.7	128.6	8.7	.58	.05		93	113.8	10.7	128.1	10.1	.53	.05
6 1/2	81	111.1	12.4	128.7	9.6	.64	.05		83	110.5	12.7	130.5	13.0	.62	.05
7 1/2	68	110.0	14.0	129.6	11.6	.51	.06		79	111.8	12.2	130.6	15.0	.41	.06
8 1/2	67	110.5	13.0	130.0	12.8	.51	.06		60	109.7	12.0	132.8	15.9	.42	.07
9 1/2	51	107.6	12.5	131.5	13.2	.53	.07		48	109.3	11.1	134.3	12.7	.29	.08
10 1/2	37	111.0	14.9	131.9	11.2	.48	.09		28	105.6	10.8	129.8	10.6	.36	.10
TOTAL SCALE															
5 1/2	84	112.8	10.8	128.6	8.7	.53	.05		93	114.1	10.4	128.1	10.1	.46	.06
6 1/2	81	111.4	10.8	128.7	9.6	.49	.06		83	114.7	10.9	130.5	13.0	.56	.05
7 1/2	68	110.8	10.9	129.6	11.6	.37	.07		79	112.8	11.0	130.6	15.0	.40	.06
8 1/2	67	111.5	10.9	130.0	12.8	.33	.08		60	112.5	10.3	132.8	15.9	.44	.07
9 1/2	51	110.2	12.8	131.5	13.2	.46	.07		48	110.1	9.9	134.3	12.7	.40	.08
10 1/2	37	110.0	11.0	131.9	11.2	.46	.09		28	107.0	9.8	129.8	10.6	.37	.10

There is also some indication of sex difference in stability of relative performance on the two subscales. Of the twelve possible comparisons for the two older groups, the correlations for the verbal scale are higher for the girls than for the boys in ten instances. The reversal of the sex trend with age is most clearly shown in the nonverbal scale. Of the six comparisons for the group 36–47 months old, the girls lead in three, the boys in three. For the oldest group of children, the boys exceed the girls in extent of correlation between the nonverbal scale and the performance test in all cases.

Arthur reports no sex differences in mean standing on the performance scale for the younger children in her group. After the age of 8 years small differences in favor of the boys are shown for most groups. Our data show a small superiority of girls over boys for both tests. This is probably due in large part to a fluctuation of sampling, although it is true that on the Minnesota scales the girls have generally been found to rank slightly higher than the boys. The difference is typically about 2 or 3 IQ-E points. Although we have been inclined to ascribe this to greater docility and better cooperation on the part of the girls, rather than to a true difference in mental level, it is possible that earlier maturation as well as general linguistic superiority may be responsible.

Putting together the evidence on sex differences in IQ stability presented in this and the preceding chapters, certain tentative conclusions seem warranted. If our cases may be looked upon as representative, it seems probable that the IQ's of girls earned before the age of 3 are slightly more predictive of later standing than are those of boys. This is consistent with the known linguistic superiority of girls at the early ages and their slightly greater maturity in other aspects of development. The indication that the sex difference in progress toward intellectual stabilization is more marked in the verbal than in the nonverbal area is also in accordance with known developmental facts. The suggestion of a shift toward greater constancy of performance among the boys after the age of 4 is not so easy to explain. Inasmuch as boys have usually been found to do better than girls on nonverbal tasks, it may be that the differential content of the test, together with increasing differentiation between the sexes in interests and aptitudes, is the explanation.

XI. PREDICTION OF STANDING ON COLLEGE ENTRANCE TESTS FROM THE MINNESOTA PRESCHOOL SCALES

FROM PRESCHOOL TO COLLEGE

Over two hundred of the children who were given the Minnesota Preschool Scales before the age of 6 have now completed high school. The University of Minnesota Testing Bureau has for some years administered the American Council on Education college entrance examinations to all Minnesota high school students toward the end of their senior year. Through the courtesy of Dr. John Darley, director of the bureau, records of our subjects who had been given these tests were made available for study.

A word of explanation is necessary before presenting the figures. In order to make these comparisons as rigid as possible, we have used only *first* administrations of the Minnesota Preschool Scales. We were interested in knowing whether or not a single test (which is all that many children ever have), when given at these early ages, shows any relationship whatever to scholastic aptitude as measured by an intelligence test designed for students entering college. We have therefore included in these comparisons not only children from the growth study for whom we have repeated measurements, but also those used only in the standardization of the scales. In order to insure identity of cases, dates of birth as well as full names, including middle names or initials when available, were cross-checked with the files in the testing bureau.

Because of the date at which our study was begun only the older and brighter children of the group have as yet been given the college ability tests. Work on the formal standardization of the Minnesota scales was started in the fall of 1927; the A.C.E. tests cover the period up to June 1941. The average age of completing high school in Minnesota is 18. Thus a very definite tendency to select the children who completed .high school before the usual age of graduation is imposed by the conditions of the investigation. For this reason we have used a somewhat different age grouping for these comparisons. Only five children who had not quite reached their third birthdays* at the time of taking the Minnesota tests could be located in the files of the testing bureau. We have included these with the 3-year-old group, here designated as the group "under 48 months." Table 36 shows the correlations of each of the three Minnesota scales with the American Council of Education test given at the close of the senior year in high school.

TABLE 36.—CORRELATIONS BETWEEN IQ-E'S ON THE MINNESOTA SCALES AND SCORES EARNED TWELVE TO FOURTEEN YEARS SUBSEQUENTLY ON THE A.C.E. COLLEGE ABILITY TESTS

Age in Months at Taking Minnesota	N	Correlation with A.C.E. Score at High School Graduation			PE of Zero r
		Verbal Scale	Nonverbal Scale	Total Scale	
Under 48	52	.00	+.08	+.12	.09
48–59	67	+.34	+.23	+.29	.08
60–72	92	+.28	+.42	+.39	.07

Only a negligible relationship between standing on the Minnesota scales before the age of 4 years and later standing on the A.C.E. tests is apparent. It must be remembered in this connection that we are dealing with a group of children all of whom were at least of sufficient ability to reach the senior year of high school at the usual age or earlier,† a fact that automatically eliminates practically all the children who were not of at least average ability. The important question is not, therefore, Do the Minnesota Preschool Scales when given before the age of 4 years distinguish between the children who at the age of 15 to 18 years will be classed as bright or dull? It is, rather, Do these scales enable us to distinguish between those who, at that later time, will show varying degrees of superiority? To the first question we have no satisfactory answer because of the difficulty of locating and retesting a sufficiently large number of our more backward cases. To the second question the answer appears to be negative. It is not immediately apparent whether the reason for the lack of predictive value within this range of talent lies

* The youngest child in this group was 33 months old when first tested.
† Inasmuch as this is the youngest age group in our study, the time restrictions bear upon them most heavily. No child in this group was as old as 18 1/2 years at the time of high school graduation; only seven of the fifty-two had passed their eighteenth birthday. In contrast three graduated at 15, sixteen at 16, and twenty-six at 17.

in the particular character of the test used or in the fact that it was the first test given and hence may have been more strongly affected by temporary emotional disturbance and other factors that would decrease its value as an index of intelligence even at the time; or whether, as accumulating evidence seems to suggest, intellectual differences at these early ages are not well stabilized. It would be possible to secure some further evidence on this point by means of a detailed analysis of results of later tests of those children for whom tests are available. Because this can be done much more adequately after the lapse of one or two years has made a larger number of children available for comparison, we are reserving this analysis for the new study mentioned in an earlier chapter.

After the age of 4 years, although the correlations remain low, they are definitely positive. Although the restriction in range of talent is not quite so great for these cases as for those first tested at an earlier age, it is still marked. In the entire list, there is no child who had reached his nineteenth birthday at the time of completing high school.

XII. SIGNIFICANCE OF A DIFFERENCE IN STANDING ON THE VERBAL AND NONVERBAL SCALES

OVERLAPPING OF THE TWO SCALES

In Chapters VI–IX inclusive it was shown that in spite of the lower weighting that has been assigned to the nonverbal scale in computing the total score, in spite of its shorter range of effectiveness, its smaller number of items and its somewhat lower reliability as computed at the time of standardization, this scale nevertheless affords a prediction of later standing on well-known tests of intelligence that is as good as or better than that provided by the verbal scale. The superiority of the nonverbal scale is marked in respect to its correlation with the two other scales making little or no demand upon language—the Merrill-Palmer and the Arthur Performance Scale—while in the case of the two revisions of the Stanford-Binet the differences are small and unreliable. Nevertheless, even for the tests in which the language factor is weighted rather heavily, the trend is similar.

This finding raises two important questions: First, to what extent do these two scales, so different in manifest content, really measure aspects of mentality that are at least partially differentiated from each other? Second, if it is found that specialized talent or, as Kelley puts it, individual idiosyncrasy, is indicated by a difference in standing on the two scales during early childhood, how persistent is this tendency? Is it purely a circumstantial affair, depending on immediate stimulation and direction of the child's interests, or is there indication of a more fundamental patterning, related perhaps to educational and vocational aptitudes that will emerge more clearly later on?

Some evidence on the first of these questions is provided by Table 37, which shows the correlations between the verbal and the nonverbal C-scores earned by the children of the standardization group after correction for attenuation. It is evident from these figures that the abilities measured by the two scales have many factors in common. Nevertheless the figures presented in Table 37 show too great and too consistent a departure from perfect correlation to support an

93

assumption that the two scales are merely different measures of the same thing. That this is not the case is further evidenced by the data reported in the preceding chapters, where it is shown that the nonverbal scale predicts later standing on other nonverbal measures far better than does the verbal scale, although the two are about equally effective in predicting later standing on the 1916 and the 1937 revisions of the Stanford-Binet, which are predominantly linguistic. It should be remembered, however, that the Stanford-Binet includes a fair proportion of nonlinguistic items and is therefore not a purely linguistic test. Yet the consistency of the results just mentioned not only tends to confirm the evidence of partial independence of the two measures given by the corrected coefficients of correlation but also points toward an affirmative answer to the second question, inasmuch as the differences in correlation appear to persist without marked change over a period of several years.

TABLE 37.—CORRELATIONS BETWEEN C-SCORES ON THE VERBAL AND NONVERBAL
SCALES CORRECTED FOR ATTENUATION

Age in Years	N	Correlations Corrected for Attenuation	Median of Two Consecutive Ages	Coefficient of Alienation
2	100	.81	. . .	. . .
2 1/2	100	1.01	.91	.41
3	100	.87	. . .	. . .
3 1/2	100	.92	.895	.45
4	100	.82	. . .	. . .
4 1/2	100	.89	.855	.52
5	100	.87	. . .	. . .
5 1/2	100	.77	.82	.57

An interesting trend shown in Table 37 is the decrease in the corrected coefficients with age, or, stated somewhat differently, the increasing differentiation between the two scores as age advances. This of course fits in very nicely with the theory of development by differentiation which, with varying degrees of qualification, is accepted by most present-day psychologists.

CORRELATION OF THE TWO SCALES WITH VOCABULARY TESTS

In the absence of a more nearly "pure" verbal test for the upper ages we have attempted various expedients by way of throwing further light on the question of the persistence of mental patterning over the years from early to later childhood and on to maturity. First, we compared the C-scores earned at various ages during the preschool years on each of the two Minnesota scales with the vocabulary scores earned on the 1916 Stanford at the age of 9 1/2. Results were as follows: For the youngest group both correlations were insignificant (+.13 for the verbal and +.05 for the nonverbal). For the group between 36 and 47 months the correlation of vocabulary with the verbal scale was +.35 and with the nonverbal +.42. For the oldest group the figures were +.25 and +.08 respectively. One would hardly be warranted in concluding from these figures that vocabulary skills at the age of 9 1/2 are better predicted by one of the Minnesota scales than by the other. Neither shows more than a slight relationship.

A similar lack of differentiation with respect to vocabulary is shown when the results of the two scales are compared with those from a vocabulary test of one hundred items given to all except two of the high school students tested by Dr. Darley (see Chapter XI). This comparison was made only for the children in the 4-year and 5-year groups. For the sixty-seven children tested between their fourth and fifth birthdays the correlations with vocabulary scores at the end of the senior year in high school were +.25 for the verbal scale and +.11 for the nonverbal scale. For the ninety children who were tested between the ages of 5 and 6 years the corresponding figures were +.33 for the verbal and +.36 for the nonverbal scale.

CORRESPONDENCE IN DIRECTION OF DIFFERENCES BETWEEN SCORES AT WIDELY SEPARATED AGES

A third procedure, however, yielded more positive results. The A.C.E. test described in Chapter XI consists of five subtests: arithmetic, artificial language, analogies, opposites, and a completion test. The last four involve the use of language in one form or another; the first appears to be the nearest available approach to a nonlinguistic test. On the assumption that the artificial-language test was perhaps the best approximation to a measure of purely linguistic skill afforded by this series, we classified our cases not on the basis of absolute score but on the basis of the direction of the difference between the two Minnesota scales on the one hand and between the artificial-language and arithmetic score on the other. The results, in terms of Chi-square value and corresponding level of significance, as read from Fisher's tables, are shown in Table 38.

TABLE 38.—CORRESPONDENCE IN DIRECTION OF THE DIFFERENCE BETWEEN VERBAL AND NONVERBAL IQ-E'S ON THE MINNESOTA SCALES AND BETWEEN THE ARITHMETIC AND THE ARTIFICIAL LANGUAGE COMPONENTS OF THE A.C.E. PSYCHOLOGICAL EXAMINATION AT THE END OF THE HIGH SCHOOL PERIOD

Age in Months at Taking Minnesota	A.C.E. Components	Verbal IQ-E Higher	Nonverbal IQ-E Higher		
Under 48	Arithmetic higher	8	14	$N = 48^*$	
	Art. Lang. higher	17	9	$Chi^2 = 4.098$ $p = 3\%$ (approx.)	
48–59	Arithmetic higher	14	9	$N = 64^*$	
	Art. Lang. higher	30	11	$Chi^2 = 1.272$ $p = 25\%$ (approx.)	
60–72	Arithmetic higher	14	25	$N = 83^*$	
	Art. Lang. higher	29	15	$Chi^2 = 6.974$ $p = $ less than 1%	

* The discrepancies between the numbers of cases included here and those reported in Chapter XI are due to the fact that in a few instances only total scores on the A.C.E. examination were available.

Although only the group first tested between the ages of 5 and 6 years shows a Chi-square value large enough (for 1 degree of freedom) to reach the 1 per cent level of significance, the same tendency is apparent at all three ages. It seems reasonably certain, therefore, that by the age of 5 years, and probably even before that time, individual differences in pattern as well as in level of ability have manifested themselves in measurable degree. These differences persist at least until the end of the high school period. In view of the fact that differential patterns of ability among high school children have been shown to bear a distinct relation to vocational aptitudes, we may perhaps not be generalizing too far beyond our data in suggesting that these differential patterns probably depend at least in part upon inherent characteristics of the individual organism.

CONCLUSIONS

Although the evidence for early differentiation in pattern as well as in level of ability that has been presented in this chapter leaves much to be desired, the data nevertheless seem to point rather definitely to the conclusion that such differentiation is manifested even before school age. Moreover, the pattern of specialized ability shown by the preschool child not only becomes more clear cut as age advances but tends to maintain its original form at least until the end of the high school period. The Minnesota Preschool Scales differentiate between two aspects only of the abilities that constitute the child's mentality. Even these differentiations are made but imperfectly. The task of outlining the faintly marked grooves in the design of the little child's mind is not an easy one, but it is worth the effort if it can be shown that the design is enduring. We believe that the Minnesota Preschool Scales provide the means for beginning such a study, but obviously much more needs to be done. The item analysis of early test results in reference to terminal status, which is now under way, should take us farther along this road.

XIII. INDIVIDUAL CASE STUDIES

The great majority of our cases show only such fluctuations in mental status from one measurement to another as may be expected to result from variations in test content at different ages, unequal degrees of cooperation on different occasions, marginal successes and failures, and similar factors that probably can never be brought under perfect control. For these children the changes in IQ from one test to another are commonly not large and show no consistent tendency.

Occasionally, however, a case is found in which the variations in standing from one occasion to another show a trend that is too consistent and too persistent to warrant explanation on the basis of chance. Our data, as well as those reported by Bayley (1940), suggest that in these cases not merely the *sign* but the *thing signified* is truly changing its level. That such changes do occur, though infrequently, has previously been suggested by Terman, Burks, and Jensen (1930).

Included in this chapter are descriptions of several cases in which the changes in IQ are small and easily accounted for by unavoidable differences in test or testing conditions from year to year, also several cases with greater changes that must be accounted for on some other basis.

CASE I (See Figure I*)

An "average" child, without consistent differentiation of ability pattern, who shows about the usual degree of fluctuation in IQ from test to test. Esther is the youngest of ten children, nine of whom are living. Her father is employed in a large industrial concern; her mother was a telephone operator before her marriage. Neither parent completed high school. All

---

* In the mental-growth charts accompanying these histories the smooth curve was derived empirically from the total C-score values at successive ages obtained from the standardization group. The formula for this curve was found to be:

$$Y = -97.2428 + 119.7371 \log X.$$

Extrapolation was carried out for the ages beyond 6 years. This procedure is open to some question but it appeared to be the soundest feasible at that time. Since the only use made of this curve is to provide a base line with which individual progress can be compared, it is unlikely that serious error has been introduced. In plotting the individual curves, C-score values have been used up to the age of 6 years, after which mental ages have been plotted directly from the corresponding chronological age levels. For the ages beyond 6 years the two revisions of the Stanford-Binet have been used as the bases for the verbal scores, the Arthur Performance Scale for the nonverbal scores. The shaded portions of the curve show the range of the middle 50 per cent of the standardization group, extrapolated for the higher ages.

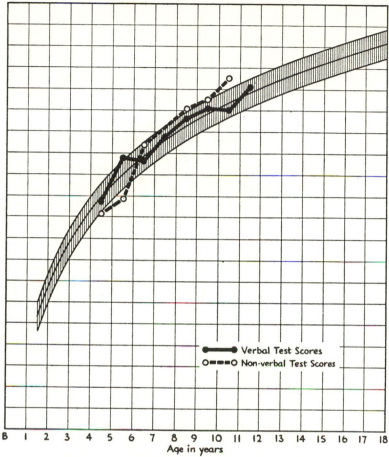

FIGURE 1.—MENTAL-GROWTH CHART FOR CASE 1

the children have made normal progress through school with the exception of one older brother who is in a special class for backward children. Esther's test results are shown below:

Age in Years	Minnesota IQ-E			Stanford IQ	Arthur IQ
	Verbal	Nonverbal	Total		
4 1/2	98	85	94	...	...
5 1/2	113	75	100	...	below norms
6 1/2	...	...	...	96 (1916)	111
7 1/2	...	...	...	102 (1916)	...
8 1/2	...	...	...	109 (1916)	113
9 1/2	...	...	...	104 (1916)	112
10 1/2	...	...	...	94 (1937 L)	124
11 1/2	...	...	...	106 (1937 M)	...

If one considers only this child's total standing on the Minnesota test, her IQ has at no time departed far from the average. During her early years the test results run somewhat lower than those earned after the age of 7 1/2, but the difference is not great. There is also a tendency for her to do better on verbal than on nonverbal tests before the age of 6 1/2, after which the reverse trend appears. It is uncertain whether or not this fact represents a genuine shift in pattern of growth; in the absence of confirmatory evidence it may be safer to attribute it to fluctuations of sampling. Except at the ages of 5 1/2 and 10 1/2, the differences in performance on the two kinds of tests are not large.

CASE 2 (See Figure 2)

A child of decidedly superior verbal ability whose nonverbal performance remains consistently at the high-average level. Jerry is the child of a traveling salesman who completed three years of college and acquired some legal training in evening classes. Jerry's mother holds an M. A. degree from a well-known eastern university. He has two younger sisters who have shown consistent high-average ability on all tests administered to them. Jerry's scores have been tabulated as follows:

Age in Years	Minnesota IQ-E			Stanford IQ	Arthur IQ
	Verbal	*Nonverbal*	*Total*		
4	127	111	122	129 (1916)	. . .
5 1/2	129	117	122	. . .	. . .
9 1/2	. . .	. . .	. . .	140 (1916)	104
11 1/2	. . .	. . .	. . .	137 (1916)	105
12 1/2	. . .	. . .	. . .	138 (1937 M)	. . .
13 1/2	. . .	. . .	. . .	149 (1937 L)	. . .

In all examinations Jerry has rated consistently lower on nonverbal than on verbal tests. He graduated from high school at the age of 16 1/2 in the seventy-third percentile of his class. His scores on the arithmetic and artificial-language components of the A.C.E. tests were 28 and 18 respectively. This is not in accordance with the pattern described in the last chapter. It must be remembered, however, that the arithmetic test is by no means an ideal measure of nonlinguistic performance. It may be of more significance to note that his total score of 76 on the vocabulary test of the Ohio

INDIVIDUAL CASE STUDIES

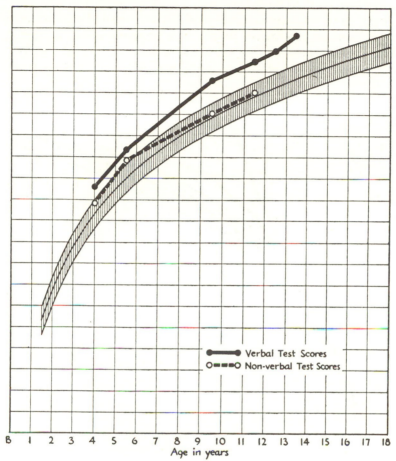

FIGURE 2.—MENTAL-GROWTH CHART FOR CASE 2

English Examination is exceeded by only six of our very superior group of cases, whereas his total score of 114 on the A.C.E. test is exceeded by sixteen other children. Inasmuch as the A.C.E. examination is also predominantly a verbal test, the fact that his relative position, though very high on both, is slightly higher on the vocabulary test alone may possibly be significant.

CASE 3 (See Figure 3)

A child who shows consistent superiority along nonverbal lines. Frances is the only child of parents who separated soon after her birth. The father was a college graduate who was not able to find permanent employment; he is listed on our records as an emergency helper in a large industrial concern. Her mother also graduated from college and taught school for a short time before her marriage. After separating from

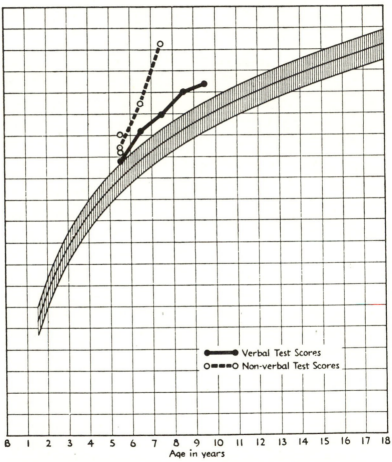

Verbal Test Scores
Non-verbal Test Scores

Age in years

FIGURE 3.—MENTAL-GROWTH CHART FOR CASE 3

her husband she took a short business course and has been employed as a stenographer since that time. Frances and her mother live with the maternal grandparents. Frances was first tested on the Minnesota scales at 5 1/2 years and at this time showed some superiority along nonverbal lines, though she scored too near the ceiling of the nonverbal scale for it to give a true indication of her nonverbal abilities. Her score on the Merrill-Palmer given at the same age was also adversely affected by the ceiling. Her rating on the Arthur test taken at the same age gives a truer picture of her nonverbal superiority:

Age in Years	Minnesota IQ-E			Merrill-Palmer IQ	Stanford IQ	Arthur IQ
	Verbal	Nonverbal	Total			
5 1/2	. . 114	129	119	125	. . .	145
6 1/2	. . . . .	. . .	. . .	. . .	127 (1916)	166
7 1/2	. . . . .	. . .	. . .	. . .	128 (1916)	199
8 1/2	. . . . .	. . .	. . .	. . .	141 (1937 L)	above norms
9 1/2	. . . . .	. . .	. . .	. . .	135 (1937 M)	. . .

Frances is a very sensitive child, somewhat shy but rather grown up in her manner of meeting new people and strange situations. This is probably partly because she has lived with adults all her life and partly because she has made many public appearances in connection with her music. She has always been very conscientious in her effort to do well on the tests and is especially enthusiastic about taking the nonverbal tests, on which she excels. Her teachers report that she does good though not outstanding work in school, receiving her best grades in arithmetic; that she is quiet, well-mannered, and if anything a little overanxious to please. She is not a popular child with her schoolmates but has several good friends among them. Most of her time outside of school is spent practicing on her violin, taking lessons, and appearing in recitals. She plays in the school orchestra and is reported to be the school's outstanding soloist. Her music teachers consider her unusually gifted in music. She has composed several violin solos which show promise.

While the Arthur scores undoubtedly have been affected by the unusual amount of practice along nonverbal lines that this child has indulged in, nevertheless, from the age of 5 1/2 her tests indicate nonverbal superiority on several different measures, a superiority borne out by her academic record since that time. It is interesting to note that the majority of items passed above her chronological age level on both the old and revised Stanford-Binet are nonverbal items, such as seeing absurdities in pictures, reproducing designs, and working out codes. Her vocabulary is only slightly above that of the average child of her age on both the 1916 Stanford-Binet and Form L of the 1937 revision.

CASE 4 (See Figure 4)

A child with an accelerating rate of mental growth, showing consistent superiority along nonverbal lines. Anna provides an excellent example of an accelerating rate of mental develop-

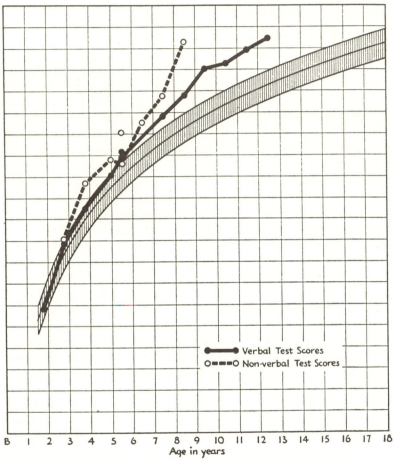

FIGURE 4.—MENTAL-GROWTH CHART FOR CASE 4

ment. Her father is a professional man of national reputation; her mother was before her marriage a clinical psychologist of extensive experience with both children and adults. Both parents hold Ph. D. degrees and have observed the development of their two children with scientific as well as personal interest.

Anna was born at full term and her early development was normal. She was a placid, good-natured baby who showed no early indications of precocity. At this time she was pronounced by both her parents to be "nice but a little stupid." This description was undoubtedly colored by comparison with her older sister, who even as an infant had shown evidences of unusually rapid development in respect to walking, talking, and other types of behavior.

Anna's scores are as follows:

| Age | Minnesota IQ-E | | | Merrill-Palmer IQ | Stanford IQ | Arthur IQ |
	Verbal	Nonverbal	Total			
1 yr., 9 mos.	98	...	98	...	...	...
2 yrs., 9 mos.	114	119	116	...	...	...
3 yrs., 10 mos.	109	136	118	...	...	...
5 yrs.	...	...	...	127	112 (1916)	...
5 yrs., 6 mos.	118	113	116	...	123 (1916)	148
6 yrs., 6 mos.	...	...	...	...	...	139
7 yrs., 6 mos.	...	...	...	...	126 (1916)	152
8 yrs., 6 mos.	...	...	...	...	133 (1916)	181
9 yrs., 6 mos.	...	...	...	...	150 (1916)	...
10 yrs., 6 mos.	...	...	...	...	143 (1916)	...
11 yrs., 6 mos.	...	...	...	...	147 (1937 L)	...
12 yrs., 6 mos.	...	...	...	...	151 (1937 M)	...

On all tests throughout the preschool period, with the exception of the Minnesota given at 66 months (when, as was pointed out in an earlier chapter, the nonverbal scale is distinctly less dependable than the verbal scale because of its lower ceiling), this child consistently ranked somewhat higher on nonverbal tasks than on verbal tasks. Moreover, if one is willing to grant some validity to the combined findings from the test given before the age of 2 years and to the parents' estimates of her ability at that time, there is at least a suggestion of unusually rapid gain in relative standing between 2 and 3 years. After that a plateau seems to have been maintained up to about the age of 5 years, when a second period of rapid growth appeared, resulting in an IQ increase of from 5 to 15 points, depending upon which measure is taken as the standard.

At 13 years and 11 months Anna was given the Ohio State Psychological Examination for college freshmen. She was then completing her sophomore year in high school. Norms for her age and grade are not available, but her score of 86 would rank her at the seventy-second percentile of Ohio

State University freshmen. Anna completed high school at the age of 16 years and 2 months, with an academic rank in the ninety-third percentile of her class. On the A.C.E. test given at the end of her senior year, her percentile rank among Minnesota high school seniors was 90.

These records seem to provide rather clear evidence of an increasing rate of mental growth with advancing age in a child who initially gave little evidence of mental precocity. In this case, moreover, the improvement seems to have come in wavelike spurts of development, followed by periods during which the IQ was maintained but showed no further increase. There is no evident discrepancy between retrospective judgment of the parents and the test records. The mother in particular states that Anna unquestionably has turned out to be much brighter than she ever anticipated she would be when she was small. The school record also tends to corroborate the results of the tests, for her work in the primary grades was only slightly above average, in a school where the average IQ is around 110, while in the upper grades and high school her standing was well toward the top in a class of very superior students.

The extremely high standing of this child on the Arthur scale should be interpreted with some qualification, inasmuch as our experience has shown that when these tests are given at annual intervals the effect of practice is very marked for bright children, although the more backward cases typically show little gain from experience. To a limited extent verbal tests also reveal this differential effect of experience, but the difference is in no way comparable to that found with the Arthur scale.

Case 5 (See Figure 5)

A child whose mental growth shows temporary arrest. Lois' father is a businessman who had one year of graduate work in college; her mother is a college graduate. She was born at full term and nothing unusual is reported about her early development. Her test results are tabulated on the next page.

When Lois took her first test at 66 months she had a noticeable speech defect. When she was given the Stanford-Binet for the first time at 78 months it was noted that she was apparently becoming more conscious of her speech difficulty

Age	Minnesota IQ-E			Stanford IQ	Arthur IQ
	Verbal	Nonverbal	Total		
5 yrs., 6 mos. . .	95	102	97	...	below norms
6 yrs., 6 mos.	...	...	...	87 (1916)	...
7 yrs., 6 mos.	...	...	...	100 (1916)	91
8 yrs., 6 mos.	...	...	...	89 (1916)	92
9 yrs., 6 mos.	...	...	...	80 (1937 L)	95
10 yrs., 6 mos.	...	...	...	74 (1937 M) 80 (1937 L)	80
11 yrs., 6 mos.	...	...	...	78 (1937 L)	...
14 yrs., 2 mos.	...	...	...	85 (1937 L)	...

and was hesitant about making verbal responses. At 10 1/2 years she was tested twice on the 1937 revision of the Stanford-Binet by different examiners who were unacquainted with each other's results. On Form M her IQ was 74; on Form L, administered four days later, it was 80; on the Arthur Performance Scale given at the same age it was also 80. She was also given the reading and arithmetic tests of the Stanford Achievement Scale at this time. On none of the four tests (paragraph meaning, 33; word meaning, 50; arithmetic reasoning, 42; and arithmetic computation, 49) did her score reach the standard for her chronological age. The most striking thing in the results of these tests is the great contrast between her performance on the more mechanical parts and on those items making greater demands on reasoning and judgment. She was at the time in grade 5B, in the slow section of her class. Even so she was unable to do satisfactory work. Her teacher reported that she was an extraordinarily hard worker who never gave any trouble along disciplinary lines.

In view of the test results it is interesting to note that the teacher who had had her in the first grade reported that "Lois was a lovely child who had no difficulty at all in learning to read. She was not the quickest in her group but neither was she in the slow group. Her speech was rather poor but improved steadily throughout the year. She wrote practically as well as the other children."

Lois has been passed along through the grades because her teachers have felt she is doing the best she can and that failure would merely discourage her from making further effort. Her articulatory difficulties still persist and a slight stutter has developed. At the time she was last seen the school reported that she was doing good work in such mechanical subjects as writing and spelling.

Examination of this child's record shows that up to about 7 1/2 years her mental-test performance varied only within the range of low-average to average ability. This is true both of the verbal and the nonverbal tests. The fact that her first-

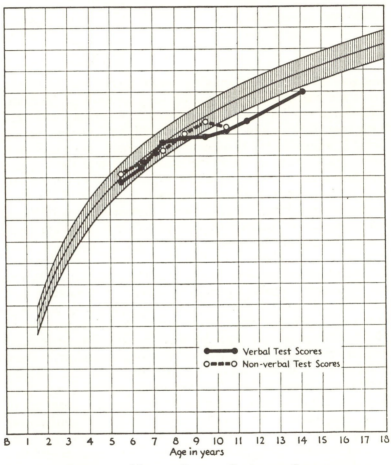

Verbal Test Scores
Non-verbal Test Scores

Age in years

FIGURE 5.—MENTAL-GROWTH CHART FOR CASE 5

grade teacher reported that her work was of approximately average quality affords some corroboration of the test results. Thereafter we have a two-year period during which there seems to have been a complete or nearly complete arrest of mental development. Then progress was again shown, though she did not make up her two-year loss. Later teachers reported her to be a hard worker but unable to keep up with the class average.

We have sought in vain for any explanation of these findings. A complete physical and neurological examination was made at the age of 10 1/2 at our recommendation, but the findings were negative. She has never had a serious illness; as a matter of fact, her health has always been better than average. Neither have there been any unusual events connected with the home or family that might be expected to arouse strong emotional reactions. Lois is the second of three children and the only girl. She quarrels with her brothers at times but apparently their differences are soon made up. The family lives in a middle-class neighborhood and is in comfortable financial circumstances, though by no means wealthy. At school Lois has always been rather a favorite with her teachers because of her good behavior and unflagging effort. She is also well liked by her classmates though she is not a leader among them.

CASE 6 (See Figure 6)

A child showing marked instability of mental-growth rate. James was first tested with the Minnesota Preschool Scales at the age of 4 1/2. The IQ's secured at that time and on follow-up tests are as follows:

Age	Minnesota IQ-E			Merrill-Palmer IQ	Stanford IQ	Arthur IQ
	Verbal	Nonverbal	Total			
4 yrs., 6 mos. . .	78	81	79	72	...	...
6 yrs.	...	...	...	...	72 (1916)	...
7 yrs., 6 mos. . .	...	...	...	...	83 (1916)	...
8 yrs., 6 mos. . .	...	...	...	...	98 (1916)	80
9 yrs., 6 mos. . .	...	...	...	...	68 (1937 L)	88
10 yrs., 1 mos. .	...	...	...	...	88 (1937 M)	...
10 yrs., 6 mos. .	...	...	...	...	89 (1937 L)	93
11 yrs., 6 mos. .	...	...	...	...	101 (1937 L)	...
12 yrs., 6 mos. .	...	...	...	...	112 (1937 M)	...

Examination of the results shows two periods of general improvement, each covering several years, with a marked slump between them. Even if we discount the one extremely low test that yielded an IQ of 68 (in the tabulation the two tests given at this time have been averaged), we still have a definite drop from the level previously attained.

From the beginning of our acquaintance with him, James's behavior has shown two outstanding characteristics: extreme over-reactivity to emotional stimuli and equally extreme pre-occupation with an inner life of fantasy. James is the oldest child in a family of three children. His two younger sisters seem normal in all respects, but from his infancy James has

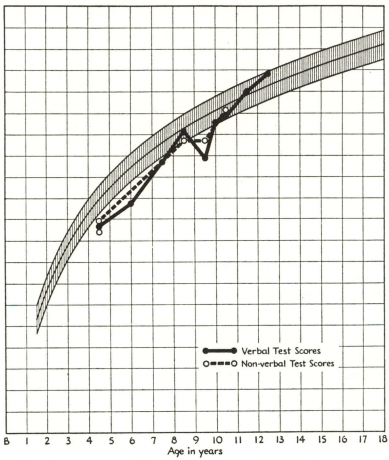

Verbal Test Scores
Non-verbal Test Scores

Age in years

FIGURE 6.—MENTAL-GROWTH CHART FOR CASE 6

been a problem. He has many fears that at times have been so extreme as to seem pathological. At the time he was first brought to us, two dogs belonging to a neighbor were causing him uncontrollable terror. After he started school the fact that he had to pass the house where the dogs were kept brought him to such a state of nervous dread (even though his mother always escorted him well past the house) that his entire system seemed to be upset. His sleep was disturbed, he was unwilling to be left alone at night, and he lost weight. The situation eventually became so serious that the family decided to move to a new neighborhood, where he was much happier. Both the nervous symptoms and his general health improved. While generalizations from this single case are certainly unwarranted, it is worth noting that the first test given after the change of residence marks the beginning of the first upward turn in his mental-test performance. The improvement continued for another year, at which time his test performance was approximately average for his age (IQ 98). However, his tendency to daydream was becoming steadily more pronounced, with the result that his school-work fluctuated greatly in quality from day to day.

At about this time a neighbor's house took fire and burned to the ground. James, along with the other members of his family, watched it. Although their own home was at no time in any danger, since the fire was actually almost two blocks distant, James became greatly excited. Shortly afterward a fire drill was held at school. James had had plenty of previous experience with fire drills, which took place, on the average, about once each month. Nevertheless, when the fire alarm sounded on this occasion he completely lost control of himself, screamed loudly, fled panic-stricken from the room, and could not be induced to go through the routine drill with the other children. From that time on, special arrangements had to be made at school for handling him during fire drills, although he was then 9 years old and in the third grade. It is noteworthy that some months later, at the time of the test on which he did so badly, he told the examiner a long tale of a terrible fire that had taken place in the neighborhood the night before. The telling was accompanied by many evidences of emotional excitement—violent gestures, dilated pupils, and so on. Nothing of the kind had occurred.

James has at all times been under excellent medical supervision. He has always tended to be underweight and to have some difficulty in sleeping. He was at one time taken to a psychiatrist for treatment but reacted in such a violently negative fashion that nothing was accomplished.

James's schoolwork has continued to be erratic up to the

present time. At the age of 11 he was transferred to a special school for underweight children, where he remained for a year. Here he seemed definitely inclined to take advantage of the greater freedom of activity to withdraw further into his own world of fantasy. Much of the time he seemed quite unaware of what was going on around him. However, he was eager for opportunities to express himself before the group and if called upon for a report on almost any topic, he would invariably turn the whole thing into an incredible story of some fantastic experience that he claimed to have had and that he would insist was true, regardless of its impossible character. His teacher felt that he was often so carried away by his own imaginings that he was truly unable to distinguish between fact and fancy.

At the time of his last test James was back in the ordinary elementary school, beginning the seventh grade. His work was still poor but better than it had been in previous years. He was still timid and played chiefly with little girls. He talked a good deal about joining a boy scout troop, but this again seemed to be a part of his fantasy life. He was much interested in religion, went to Sunday school regularly, and talked of his plans for becoming a minister when he grows up.

To what extent the marked variations in James's test performance represent real changes in his ability is questionable. The most probable conclusion seems to be that they reflect genuine, but largely emotionally determined, shifts in his ability to organize his mental powers for the task at hand. It will be interesting to see whether or not the extreme emotional instability and quasi-psychotic behavior that have characterized this boy's childhood will crystallize into definite mental disorder when he grows up.

XIV. SUMMARY AND CONCLUSIONS

Prospect versus Retrospect

Almost fourteen years have elapsed since the first steps in the construction of the Minnesota Preschool Scales were taken. That changes in our point of view toward tests and testing should have occurred since that time is natural, perhaps inevitable. Certainly such changes have taken place. It seems pertinent, therefore, in concluding this report, to devote a few paragraphs to the contrast between our earlier concepts and those that have emerged as a result of more recent studies by ourselves and by our contemporaries.

Even as early as 1928 the distinction between measurement and prediction of mental growth had been explicitly made by Goodenough in her study of the Kuhlmann-Binet tests. It was also noted at that time that the correlation between earlier status and growth increment, especially during the early years of rapid mental development, is probably much lower than the correlations between tests and retests of school children had led many to suppose. It was likewise pointed out that the overlapping of measurements from age to age is an adequate explanation of a fairly large proportion of the correlations between repeated measures of the same individual. The phrase *constancy of the IQ* does not necessarily mean constancy of growth rate. These points have since been more completely brought out by Anderson (1939).

The findings of the present study, together with recent reports from other laboratories, have shown rather clearly that the suggestions tentatively put forth more than a decade ago were well founded. We may now say with reasonable assurance that over and above the errors of measurement that unquestionably occur, individual mental growth does not always proceed at a fixed and uniform rate. Its course is likely to be more or less irregular, particularly at the early ages. The method of computing the IQ inevitably smooths out these irregularities to some extent, just as the application of a moving average smooths out the irregularities in a learning curve. As in the latter instance, the procedure has been justified on the ground that the irregularities so eliminated are merely chance fluctuations that obscure the general trend. Within limits this is undoubtedly true, but it is stretching the limits of coincidence too far to attribute to mere accidents of testing, growth trends which persist without material change in direction over as long periods as those reported in a number of the cases studied in the preceding chapter. These cases, it should be noted, are not highly unusual, though the specimens chosen have been selected as rather clear-cut examples of the types that it was desired to illustrate. Our files contain many others equally striking.

It is well, however, once more to stress the fact that cases showing marked and consistent shifts in standing, even though they occur too often to be ignored, are nevertheless exceptional rather than typical. For the vast majority of children, consistency rather than inconsistency of mental progress is the rule. Particularly when children are small and easily upset, even a very marked difference in the test results obtained on two different occasions should be interpreted conservatively and not necessarily regarded as indicating a real change in mental ability. Even when there is sufficient reason for concluding that the developmental tempo of a particular child was initially slow but accelerated later, or showed an early precocity that was not maintained, we must be cautious in assigning a cause for such deviations from the usual pattern. We know that similar aberrations appear in physical growth and not always for the same apparent reasons. Sometimes they seem to arise from external causes; in other cases constitutional factors, often of a familial nature, seem responsible. Because of the difficulty of knowing all the facts relating to an individual case, anatomists have wisely been hesitant in assuming causes for observed changes in rate of physical growth or in prescribing rules by which growth may be retarded or accelerated.

The same principles apply in the area of mental growth. There is no logical or biological reason for assuming that changes in growth tempo, even though there is reason for believing them to be genuine, are always and of necessity induced by some external influence. There is even less reason for assuming that all changes in test standing truly signify corresponding changes in mental level.

It may thus be said that as far as many of the major issues are concerned, our present concepts of mental growth do not differ greatly from those held earlier, except that we are now able to present more conclusive evidence in their support. The changes in viewpoint that were mentioned earlier may be summarized rather briefly as follows:

It has grown increasingly clear that the methods of appraising the abilities of infants and very young children that looked so promising more than a decade ago were not well chosen. It is now apparent that one of two things must be true. Either there are no infantile behavioral manifestations by which later mental progress can be usefully predicted or those that have been traditionally depended upon are misleading and should be disregarded in favor of a new and hitherto neglected series. Even the conventional indications of brightness in children of nursery school age have only moderate value in predicting terminal mental status. Fourteen years ago, in common with many if not most other psychologists, we were of the opinion that the prediction of ultimate mental status, even before the age of two years, was an objective not far beyond our grasp. Now it would be more accurate to describe it as a hope not completely relinquished.

Fourteen years ago we should have been much more skeptical than we are at present about the possibility of discovering and measuring early specialization of abilities. Although little consideration had then been given to the matter,* our feeling at that time was that, whereas small children unquestionably differed in their interests and, temporarily at least, in the kind of tasks at which they excelled, these differences were for the most part circumstantial variations within a relatively amorphous whole. In devising the verbal and the nonverbal parts of the Minnesota Preschool Scales we were motivated chiefly by the desire to provide two different means of approach to the child's mentality rather than to measure two different aspects of his ability. The comparatively high correlation between the two scales for the standardization group, even though those correlations fell short of unity, tended to confirm our impression of the relatively undifferentiated character of the child mind. Least of all did we anticipate that variations in type of ability shown during preschool years would be significantly related to later mental

---

* Some work on intra-individual differences in ability had appeared at that time, but this research was based on studies of achievement in grade school children.

idiosyncrasies. The finding that a relationship between early and later mental pattern may possibly be almost as clearly marked as that between early and later mental level is, in our opinion, one of the most significant results of the present study. Whether or not this is actually the case can, of course, only be determined with certainty when more discriminating measures for the study of mental idiosyncrasy during early years have been developed.

Fourteen years ago the question of sex differences in mental traits was largely confined to the two aspects of relative level and relative variability. Both these factors depend upon the content of the test used; hence no generalized statement on the subject is warranted. Yet our findings have raised another question: Is there a sex difference in the rate of stabilization of mental ability? Most investigations have shown some feminine precocity in respect to such infantile skills as walking and talking. Our results suggest the possibility that a similar difference may exist in respect to the age at which mental tests begin to have predictive value for later intellectual standing as well as the possibility that a reversal of this early sex trend may appear later on. Certainly both of these results need confirmation from other sources before they can be accepted as final. It is to be hoped that in future studies on the prediction of later from earlier mental status the question of a possible sex difference in correlational tendency will be taken into account.

LOOKING TO THE FUTURE

As is usual in research, we bring this report to a close with the feeling that it has suggested more questions than it has answered. For some of these questions the further analyses of our data, now under way, may provide an answer.

The fact that our correlations between first test and later standing show only a slight tendency to change with the interval between tests (although there is the usual marked relationship to age at first testing) suggests that the factor of overlapping functions may be distinctly less important in reducing the correlation between test and retest than has been thought. It is possible that a maturational factor which, for want of a better name, we may call the *level of mental stabilization* far outweighs the factor of overlap. If this is the case, then Anderson's (1939) suggestion that much improvement in the predictive value of tests for young children might be brought about by means of an item analysis in which terminal rather than initial status is used as one of the criteria for selection is pertinent.

By the time this monograph is printed, another group of our subjects will have completed high school. These cases will by then have come so close to mental maturity that the small increment still to be attained may safely be ignored. Adding the new cases to the group of over two hundred who have already finished high school should provide us with from three hundred to four hundred subjects for study. We plan to compare success or failure on each item of the Minnesota Preschool Scales and on other tests given during the preschool years with terminal ability as indicated by the tests given at the completion of high school. It is quite obvious that such a plan would have been impossible fourteen years ago, since the necessary data were not then available. Perhaps the chief value of this first study has consisted in providing the data for a second.

Another question for which our present data can furnish at least a partial answer has to do with the sex difference mentioned in a preceding chapter. In this report we have confined ourselves to a comparison of the results obtained from the first Minnesota test with those from later tests of the same children. We decided upon this limitation in the present report because of the repeated showing that experience in taking tests has a distinct effect not only upon mean standing but even more upon the correlation between tests. The increase in correlation is in part attributable to greater ease on the part of the test-wise child. In part it may be due to memory factors, especially when the tests are separated by only a short interval of time.* In part it may be the result of minor variations in test procedures on the part of examiners who are acquainted with the results of previous testings. This unconscious tendency to force the results of the tests to con-

---

* There is evidence that memory of certain items may persist over a considerable period, at least with children of school age. We have found that our own children not infrequently make such comments as "Oh, yes, I remember; I did that last year," when being retested after a year's interval with the 1916 Stanford-Binet or other tests having but a single form. As has been mentioned elsewhere, the effect of previous experience is particularly marked in the case of the Arthur Performance Scale.

form to "child reputation" is in our opinion a far more potent element in producing correlation between tests than many have supposed. Whatever may be the relative importance of these factors, it can readily be shown that test-retest correlations are in most cases distinctly higher when based upon children who have had previous experience in taking tests than when derived from naïve subjects. Inasmuch as the great majority of children examined for clinical reasons rather than for purposes of research receive but a single test, we have thought it well to report, as a rule, only the correlations derived from the first test.* Obviously, however, the correlations between tests other than the Minnesota scales administered at the later ages are suitable for the study of sex difference. Such a study will very shortly be undertaken by a member of our staff. Apart from the question of sex difference, these results will have value in testing certain statistical formulas recently proposed by Anderson (1939) and by Roff (1941).

The need for further investigation on the question of early specialization of mental ability is clearly shown by our data. The material we now have is probably not extensive enough to serve the purpose of anything more than a preliminary study, but it will at least provide the nucleus for such a study and may perhaps be sufficient to outline a plan for future work. Nevertheless the relatively clear differentiation of verbal from nonverbal abilities revealed by our data justifies the hope that other factors may also be distinguishable at an age much earlier than that at which the study of special talent has usually been undertaken. Perhaps a factorial analysis of responses on the twenty-five groups of items in the Minnesota scales might serve as a starting point.

These are but a few of the many unsolved problems and uncompleted tasks that call for further study. The opinion is sometimes expressed that since mental testing reached a stage of practical usefulness and gained a position of scientific respectability more than a quarter of a century ago, the really significant problems pertaining to the field have all been solved. On the contrary, as far as the early stages of mental development are concerned, these problems are only now beginning to emerge.

* In Chapter VI, which deals with correlations between earlier and later testings on the Minnesota scales, results of retests are also shown.

APPENDIX

IQ-Equivalents for the Merrill-Palmer Tests

(For the method of derivation see page 66.)

CA in Months										Number of Items Passed													
	3	4	5	6	7	8	9	10	11	12	13	14	15	16	17	18	19	20	21	22	23	24	25
18	100	101	102	103	104	105	106	107	108	109	110	110	111	112	113	114	115	116	117	118	119	120	121
19	99	100	100	101	102	103	104	105	106	107	108	109	110	111	111	112	113	114	115	116	117	118	119
20	98	98	100	100	100	101	102	103	104	105	106	107	108	109	110	110	111	112	113	114	115	116	117
21	95	96	97	98	99	100	101	102	103	104	105	106	107	108	109	110	110	111	112	113	114	115	116
22	94	95	96	97	98	99	100	100	101	102	103	104	105	106	107	108	109	110	110	111	112	113	114
23	92	93	94	95	96	97	98	99	100	100	101	102	103	104	105	106	107	108	109	110	110	111	112
24	90	90	91	92	93	94	95	96	97	98	100	100	101	102	102	103	104	105	106	107	108	109	110
25	90	89	90	90	91	92	93	93	94	95	96	98	99	100	100	100	101	103	103	105	106	107	108
26	88	88	88	89	90	91	91	92	93	94	95	96	97	98	99	100	100	101	102	103	104	105	106
27	86	87	86	87	88	89	90	90	91	92	93	94	95	96	97	98	99	100	100	101	102	103	104
28	84	85	86	85	86	87	88	89	90	90	91	92	93	94	95	96	97	98	98	99	100	101	102
29	82	83	82	83	84	85	86	87	88	89	90	90	91	92	93	94	95	96	97	98	99	100	100
30	80	81	82	81	82	83	84	85	86	87	88	89	90	90	91	92	93	94	95	96	97	98	99
31	78	79	80	78	79	80	81	82	83	84	85	86	87	88	89	90	90	91	92	93	94	95	96
32	76	78	77	78	77	77	78	79	80	81	82	83	84	85	86	87	88	89	90	90	91	92	93
33	75	76	74	75	76	75	76	77	78	79	80	81	82	83	84	85	86	87	88	89	90	90	91
34	73	73	72	73	74	72	73	74	75	76	77	78	79	80	81	82	82	83	84	85	86	87	88
35	72	71	70	70	71	70	71	72	73	74	75	76	77	78	79	80	81	81	82	83	84	85	86
36	70	69	70	69	70	69	70	70	71	72	73	74	75	76	77	78	76	77	78	79	80	81	85
37	68	67	68	67	70	66	67	68	69	70	71	71	72	73	74	75	73	74	75	76	77	78	82
38	66	65	65	64	68	63	64	65	66	67	70	69	71	70	70	72	71	73	73	74	75	76	79
39	64	62	63	61	65	62	62	64	62	65	68	67	70	69	70	70	70	71	72	73	73	74	77
40	61	59	60	59	62	61	60	63	66	63	66	65	68	67	68	69	69	70	70	71	72	73	75
41	58	57	58	57	60	59	59	61	61	62	64	64	66	66	67	68	67	68	69	70	70	71	74
42	56	56	55	56	58	58	57	60	61	61	63	62	65	64	65	66	66	67	68	69	70	70	72
43	54	54	55	54	57	56	56	58	60	60	61	61	63	63	64	64	65	66	67	67	70	70	71
44	53	53	54	53	55	55	54	57	59	59	60	59	62	61	62	63	63	64	65	66	67	69	70
45	51	52	52	51	54	53	53	56	58	57	58	58	60	60	61	62	61	62	63	65	65	68	69
46	50	51	51	50	53	52	51	54	57	56	57	56	59	58	59	60	59	61	61	64	63	66	67
47	49	49	50	50	51	51	50	53	55	55	55	55	57	55	58	58	58	60	60	62	62	64	65
48	48	47	48	47	50	50	49	52	53	54	52	54	55	53	56	56	57	59	58	61	60	63	64
49	46	46	46	46	48	48	47	51	52	52	49	53	54	51	54	55	56	58	56	60	58	61	62
50	44	45	45	44	47	46	45	50	50	51	48	51	50	50	53	53	54	57	55	59	57	60	60
51	44	44	44	44	45	44	44	48	47	50	47	50	49	49	51	51	52	55	54	57	56	58	59
52	43	43	43	42	43	43	43	46	46	48	46	49	48	47	50	50	51	54	53	56	54	57	58
53	41	42	41	41	42	42	42	45	45	47	45	48	47	45	49	49	50	53	52	55	53	56	57
54		40	40	40	41	41	41	44	44	46	44	47	44	44	48	48	50	52	51	54	52	55	56
55					40	40	40	43	43	44	42	46	43	43	46	46	48	51	51	53	51	54	55
56								42	41	42	41	45	42	42	45	45	47	50	50	52	50	53	54
57								41	40	41	40	43	41	41	44	44	45	49	49	51	49	51	52
58										40		42	40	40	43	43	45	48	48	50	50	50	51
59												41			42	42	44	47	47	50	49	50	50
60												40			41	41	43	46	46	48	48	49	49
61															40	40	42	45	45	47	47	48	48
62																		44	44	46	46	48	49
63																		43	44	45	46	47	48

Number of Items Passed

CA in Months	26	27	28	29	30	31	32	33	34	35	36	37	38	39	40	41	42	43	44	45	46	47	48
18	122	123	124	125	126	127	128	129	130	130	131	132	133	134	135	136	137	138	139	140	141	142	143
19	120	121	122	123	124	125	126	127	128	129	130	131	131	132	133	134	135	136	137	138	139	140	141
20	118	119	120	121	122	123	124	125	126	127	128	129	130	130	131	132	133	134	135	136	137	138	139
21	117	118	119	120	121	122	123	124	125	126	127	128	129	130	130	131	132	133	134	135	136	137	138
22	115	116	117	118	119	120	121	122	123	124	125	126	127	128	129	130	130	131	132	133	134	135	136
23	113	114	115	116	117	118	119	120	121	122	123	124	125	126	127	128	129	130	130	131	132	133	134
24	112	113	114	115	116	117	118	119	120	121	122	123	124	125	126	127	128	129	130	130	131	132	133
25	110	111	112	113	114	115	116	117	118	119	120	121	122	123	124	125	126	127	128	129	130	130	131
26	109	110	110	111	112	113	114	115	116	117	118	119	120	121	122	123	124	125	126	127	128	129	130
27	107	108	109	110	110	111	112	113	114	115	116	117	118	119	120	121	122	123	124	125	126	127	128
28	105	106	107	108	109	110	110	111	112	113	114	115	116	117	118	119	120	121	122	123	124	125	126
29	103	104	105	106	107	108	109	110	110	111	112	113	114	115	116	117	118	119	120	121	122	123	124
30	101	102	103	104	105	106	107	108	109	110	110	111	112	113	114	115	116	117	118	119	120	121	122
31	100	100	100	101	102	103	104	105	106	107	108	109	109	110	111	112	113	114	115	116	117	118	119
32	97	98	99	100	100	100	101	102	103	104	105	106	107	108	109	110	110	111	112	113	114	115	116
33	94	95	96	97	98	99	100	100	101	102	103	104	105	106	107	108	109	110	110	111	112	113	114
34	92	93	94	95	96	97	98	99	100	101	102	102	103	104	105	106	106	107	108	109	110	110	111
35	90	91	92	93	94	96	97	98	99	100	101	101	102	103	104	105	105	106	107	108	109	109	110
36	88	89	90	91	92	93	94	95	96	97	98	99	100	100	101	102	103	104	105	106	107	107	108
37	86	87	88	89	90	91	92	93	94	95	96	97	98	98	99	100	101	101	102	103	104	104	105
38	83	84	85	86	88	89	90	91	92	93	94	94	95	96	96	97	98	98	99	100	101	101	102
39	80	81	82	83	84	86	87	88	89	90	91	92	93	93	94	95	96	96	97	98	99	99	100
40	78	79	80	82	83	85	86	87	88	89	90	91	92	92	93	94	95	95	96	97	98	98	99
41	76	77	79	80	81	83	84	85	86	87	88	89	90	90	91	92	93	93	94	95	96	96	97
42	75	76	77	78	79	81	82	83	84	85	86	87	88	89	89	90	91	92	93	94	95	95	96
43	73	74	76	77	78	80	81	82	83	84	85	86	87	87	88	89	90	90	91	92	93	93	94
44	72	73	74	75	76	78	79	80	81	82	83	84	85	86	86	87	88	89	90	91	92	92	93
45	70	71	73	74	75	77	78	79	80	81	82	83	84	84	85	86	87	87	88	89	90	90	91
46	70	71	72	73	74	75	76	77	78	79	80	81	82	83	83	84	85	86	87	88	89	89	90
47	68	69	70	71	72	74	75	76	77	78	79	80	81	82	82	83	84	85	86	87	88	88	89
48	66	67	68	69	70	72	73	74	75	76	77	78	79	80	80	81	82	83	84	85	86	86	87
49	65	66	67	68	69	70	71	72	73	74	75	76	77	78	79	80	81	82	83	84	85	85	86
50	63	64	65	66	67	69	70	71	72	73	74	75	76	77	77	78	79	80	81	82	83	83	84
51	61	62	63	64	65	67	68	69	70	71	72	73	74	75	75	76	77	78	79	80	81	81	82
52	60	61	62	63	64	66	67	68	69	70	71	72	73	74	74	75	76	77	78	79	80	80	81
53	59	60	61	62	63	65	66	67	68	69	70	71	72	73	73	74	75	76	77	78	79	79	80
54	58	59	60	61	62	64	65	66	67	68	69	70	71	72	72	73	74	75	76	77	78	78	79
55	57	58	59	60	61	63	64	65	66	67	68	69	70	70	71	72	73	73	74	75	76	76	77
56	56	57	58	59	60	62	63	64	65	66	67	68	69	69	70	71	72	72	73	74	75	75	76
57	54	55	56	57	58	59	60	61	62	63	64	65	66	67	68	69	70	71	72	73	74	74	75
58	53	54	55	56	57	58	59	60	61	62	63	64	65	66	67	68	69	70	71	72	73	73	74
59	52	53	54	55	56	57	58	59	60	61	62	63	64	65	66	67	68	69	70	71	72	72	73
60	51	52	53	54	55	56	57	58	59	60	61	62	63	64	65	66	67	68	69	70	71	71	72
61	50	51	52	53	54	55	56	57	58	59	60	61	62	63	64	65	66	67	68	69	70	70	71
62	50	50	51	52	53	54	55	56	57	58	59	60	61	62	63	64	65	66	67	68	69	69	70
63	49	49	50	51	52	53	54	55	56	57	58	59	60	61	62	63	64	65	66	67	68	69	70

CA in Months	49	50	51	52	53	54	55	56	57	58	59	60	61	62	63	64	65	66	67	68	69	70	71
18	144	145	146	147	148	149	150	150	151	152	153	154	155	156	157	158	159	160	159	160		160	160
19	142	143	144	145	146	147	148	149	150	150	151	152	153	154	155	156	157	158	157	158	159	159	158
20	140	141	142	143	144	145	146	147	148	149	150	150	151	152	153	154	155	156	156	157	158	157	156
21	139	140	141	142	143	144	145	146	147	148	149	150	150	151	152	153	154	155	154	155	156	155	155
22	137	138	139	140	141	142	143	144	145	146	147	148	149	150	150	151	152	153	152	153	154	154	153
23	135	136	137	138	139	140	141	142	143	144	145	146	147	148	149	150	151	151	151	152	153	152	151
24	134	135	136	137	138	139	140	141	142	143	144	145	146	147	148	149	150	150	150	150	151	150	150
25	132	133	134	135	136	137	138	139	140	141	142	143	144	145	146	147	148	149	148	149	150	149	148
26	130	131	132	133	134	135	136	137	138	139	140	141	142	143	144	145	146	147	146	147	148	147	146
27	129	130	130	131	132	133	134	135	136	137	138	139	140	141	142	143	144	145	144	145	146	145	144
28	127	128	129	130	130	131	132	133	134	135	136	137	138	139	140	141	142	143	142	143	144	143	141
29	125	126	127	128	129	130	130	131	132	133	134	135	136	137	138	139	140	141	140	141	142	140	138
30	123	123	122	126	127	128	129	130	130	131	132	133	134	135	136	137	138	139	137	138	139	137	136
31	120	121	122	123	124	125	126	127	128	129	130	130	131	132	133	134	135	136	134	135	136	135	133
32	117	118	119	120	121	122	123	124	125	126	127	128	129	130	130	131	132	133	132	133	134	132	131
33	115	116	117	118	119	120	121	122	123	124	125	126	127	128	129	130	130	131	130	130	131	130	130
34	112	113	114	115	116	117	118	119	120	121	122	123	124	125	126	127	128	129	128	129	130	129	127
35	110	111	112	113	114	115	116	117	118	119	120	121	122	123	124	125	126	127	126	127	128	126	124
36	109	110	110	111	112	113	114	115	116	117	118	119	120	121	122	123	124	125	124	125	125	123	122
37	106	107	108	109	110	110	111	112	113	114	115	116	117	118	119	120	121	122	121	122	122	121	120
38	103	104	105	106	107	108	109	110	110	111	112	113	114	115	116	117	118	119	118	119	120	119	119
39	101	102	103	104	105	106	107	108	109	110	111	111	112	113	114	115	116	117	116	117	118	118	117
40	100	100	101	102	103	104	105	106	107	108	109	110	110	111	112	113	114	115	114	116	117	116	116
41	98	100	100	101	102	103	104	105	106	107	108	109	110	110	111	112	113	114	113	114	115	115	114
42	97	98	100	100	100	101	102	103	104	105	106	107	108	110	110	110	111	112	111	113	114	113	113
43	95	97	99	99	100	100	101	102	103	104	105	106	107	108	109	110	110	111	110	111	112	112	111
44	94	96	97	98	99	99	100	100	101	102	103	104	105	106	106	108	109	110	109	110	111	110	111
45	92	95	96	97	97	97	98	99	100	101	102	103	104	105	104	107	108	109	107	109	110	109	110
46	91	93	94	95	96	96	97	98	99	100	100	100	102	103	102	105	106	107	106	107	108	108	109
47	90	92	93	94	94	94	95	96	97	98	99	100	100	101	100	103	104	105	104	106	107	106	107
48	88	90	91	92	93	92	93	94	95	96	97	98	99	100	100	102	103	104	103	104	105	104	105
49	87	89	90	90	91	91	92	93	94	95	96	97	98	99	99	100	101	102	101	103	103	103	104
50	85	88	89	90	90	90	90	91	92	93	94	95	96	97	98	99	100	101	100	102	102	102	103
51	83	86	87	88	89	88	89	90	91	91	93	93	94	95	96	97	99	100	100	101	101	101	102
52	82	84	85	86	87	87	88	89	90	90	91	92	93	94	95	96	98	99	99	100	100	100	101
53	81	83	84	85	86	86	87	88	89	89	90	91	92	93	94	95	97	98	98	99	99	99	100
54	80	82	83	84	85	85	86	87	88	88	90	90	91	92	93	94	96	97	97	98	98	97	98
55	79	81	82	83	84	84	85	86	87	87	89	89	90	91	92	93	95	96	96	97	96	96	97
56	78	80	81	82	83	83	84	85	86	86	88	88	89	90	91	92	94	95	95	95	95	95	96
57	76	79	80	81	80	81	82	83	84	85	86	87	88	89	90	90	92	93	93	94	94	94	95
58	75	77	78	79	79	80	81	82	83	84	85	86	87	88	89	90	91	92	92	93	93	93	94
59	74	76	77	78	78	79	80	81	82	83	84	85	86	87	88	89	90	91	91	92	92	92	93
60	73	75	76	77	77	78	79	80	81	82	83	84	85	86	87	88	89	90	90	91	91	91	92
61	72	74	75	76	76	77	78	79	80	81	82	83	84	85	86	87	88	89	89	90	90	90	91
62	71	73	74	75	75	76	77	78	79	80	81	82	83	84	85	86	87	88	88	90	90		
63	70	71	72	73	74	75	76	77	78	79	80	81	82	83	84	85	86	87	88	89	90		

CA in Months	72	73	74	75	76	77	78	79	80	81	82	83	84	85	86	87	88	89	90	91	92	93
18																						
19																						
20			159																			
21		160	158																			
22	159	158	156																			
23	157	157	154	160	160																	
24	156	155	152	157	158	159	160															
25	154	153	150	154	155	156	157	159	160													
26	152	151	149	151	153	154	155	157	158	159	160											
27	150	150	147	149	150	151	152	154	155	156	157	159	160									
28	149	148	144	146	147	149	150	152	153	154	155	156	157	159	160							
29	147	146	142	143	145	146	147	148	150	151	152	153	154	156	157	159	160					
30	145	143	139	140	142	143	144	145	147	148	149	150	152	153	154	155	157	158	159			
31	142	140	137	138	139	141	142	143	144	145	147	148	149	150	151	153	154	155	157	160	159	
32	139	138	134	135	137	138	139	140	142	143	144	145	147	148	149	150	152	153	154	158	156	160
33	137	135	132	133	135	136	137	138	140	141	142	143	145	146	147	148	150	151	152	155	153	157*
34	134	133	130	131	133	134	135	136	138	139	140	141	143	144	145	146	148	149	150	152	151	154*
35	132	131	128	129	130	132	133	134	135	136	138	139	140	141	142	144	145	146	148	150	150	152*
36	130	129	126	127	128	129	131	132	133	134	135	136	137	138	140	141	142	143	145	149	147	150*
37	128	126	124	125	126	127	129	130	131	132	133	134	135	136	138	139	140	141	142	146	144	148*
38	125	124	122	123	124	125	127	128	129	130	131	132	133	134	136	137	138	139	140	143	142	145*
39	123	123	121	122	123	124	126	127	128	129	130	131	132	133	135	136	137	138	138	141	140	143*
40	121	122	120	121	122	123	124	125	126	127	129	130	131	132	133	134	135	136	137	139	139	141*
41	120	121	118	119	120	121	123	124	125	126	127	128	129	130	132	133	134	135	135	138	137	140*
42	118	119	117	118	119	120	121	122	123	124	126	127	128	129	130	131	132	133	134	136	136	138*
43	117	118	116	117	118	119	120	121	122	123	125	126	127	128	129	130	131	132	132	135	134	137*
44	115	116	114	115	116	117	118	119	120	121	123	124	125	126	127	128	129	130	131	133	133	135*
45	114	115	113	114	115	116	117	118	119	120	122	123	124	125	126	127	128	129	130	132	131	134*
46	112	113	112	113	114	115	116	117	118	119	120	121	122	123	124	125	126	127	128	131	130	132*
47	111	112	110	111	112	113	114	115	116	117	119	120	121	122	123	124	125	126	127	129	129	130*
48	110	110	109	110	111	112	113	114	115	116	117	118	119	120	121	122	123	124	125	128	127	130*
49	108	109	108	109	110	111	112	113	114	115	116	117	118	119	120	121	122	123	124	126	125	128*
50	106	107	107	108	109	110	111	112	113	114	115	116	117	118	119	120	121	122	123	124	124	126*
51	105	106	106	107	108	109	110	111	112	113	114	115	116	117	118	119	120	121	122	123	123	125*
52	104	104	105	106	107	108	109	110	111	112	113	114	115	116	117	118	119	120	121	122	122	124*
53	103	104	104	105	106	107	108	109	110	111	112	113	114	115	116	117	118	119	120	121	121	123*
54	102	103	103	104	105	106	107	108	109	110	110	111	112	113	114	115	116	117	118	120	120	122*
55	100	102	102	103	104	105	106	107	108	109	109	110	111	112	113	114	115	116	117	119	118	121*
56	99	101	101	102	103	104	105	106	107	108	108	109	110	111	112	113	114	115	116	117	117	119*
57	98	100	100	101	102	103	104	105	106	107	107	108	109	110	111	112	113	114	115	116	116	118*
58	97	99	99	100	101	102	103	104	105	106	106	107	108	109	110	111	112	113	114	115	115	117*
59	96	98	98	99	100	101	102	103	104	105	105	106	107	108	109	110	111	112	113	114	114	116*
60	95	97	97	98	99	100	101	102	103	104	104	105	106	107	108	109	110	111	112	113	113	115*
61	94	96	96	97	98	99	100	101	102	103	103	104	105	106	107	108	109	110	111	112	112	114*
62	93	94	95	96	97	98	99	100	101	102	103	104	105	106	107	108	109	110	111	111	111	113*
63	92	93	94	95	96	97	98	99	100	101	102	103	104	105	106	107	108	109	110	110	111	112*

* Or higher. Because of the limits of the scale, IQ-E's are necessarily underestimates for children of 33 months or over who pass all the items.

BIBLIOGRAPHY

ANDERSON, J. E. 1939. The limitations of infant and preschool tests in the measurement of intelligence. Journal of Psychology, 8:351-79.

ARTHUR, G. 1930. A point scale of performance tests. Vol. I. Clinical manual. New York: Commonwealth Fund, Division of Publications. x, 82 pp.

———— 1933. A point scale of performance tests. Vol. II. The process of standardization. New York: Commonwealth Fund, Division of Publications. xi, 106 pp.

ARTHUR, G., and H. WOODROW. 1919. An absolute intelligence scale: a study in method. Journal of Applied Psychology, 3:118-37.

ATKINS, R. E. 1931. The measurement of the intelligence of young children by an object-fitting test. Minneapolis: University of Minnesota Press. 39 pp.

BAYLEY, N. 1933. Mental growth during the first three years: a developmental study of sixty-one children by repeated tests. Genetic Psychology Monographs, 14:1-85.

———— 1939. The predictive value of several different measures of mental growth during the first nine years. Psychological Bulletin, 36:571-72.

———— 1940a. Mental growth in young children. Thirty-Ninth Yearbook of the National Society for the Study of Education (Intelligence: Its Nature and Nurture), Part II, pp. 11-47. Bloomington, Illinois: Public School Publishing Company.

———— 1940b. Factors influencing the growth of intelligence in young children. Thirty-Ninth Yearbook of the National Society for the Study of Education (Intelligence: Its Nature and Nurture), Part II, pp. 49-79. Bloomington, Illinois: Public School Publishing Company.

BINET, A. 1911. La mésure du développement de l'intelligence chez les jeunes enfants. Société pour l'étude psychologique de l'enfant, 11:187-248.

BINET, A., and T. SIMON. 1905. Méthodes nouvelles pour le diagnostic du niveau intellectuel des anormaux. L'Année psychologique, 11:191-244.

———— 1908. Le développement de l'intelligence chez les enfants. L'Année psychologique, 14:1-94.

BIRD, G. 1923. Rhode Island kindergarten test. Bloomington: Public School Publishing Company.

BROWN, R. W. 1933. The time interval between test and retest in its relation to the constancy of the intelligence quotient. Journal of Educational Psychology, 24:81-96.

BÜHLER, C. 1930. The first year of life. Translated by P. Greenberg and H. Ripin. New York: John Day Company. x, 281 pp.

BÜHLER, C., and H. HETZER. 1932. Kleinkindertests: Tests von 1 bis 6 Lebensjahr. Leipzig: Barth. vi, 188 pp.

———— 1935. Testing children's development from birth to school age. Translated by H. Beaumont. New York: Farrar and Rinehart. 191 pp.

CATTELL, PSYCHE. 1940. The measurement of intelligence of infants and young children. New York: Psychological Corporation. 274 pp.

CHAILLE, S. E. 1887. Infants, their chronological progress. New Orleans Medical and Surgical Journal, 14:893-912.

DRISCOLL, G. P. 1933. The developmental status of the preschool child as a prognosis of future development. New York: Bureau of Publications, Teachers College, Columbia University. 111 pp.

EBERT, E. H. 1941. A comparison of the original and revised Stanford-Binet scales. Journal of Psychology, 11:47-61.

ENGEL, A. M., and H. J. BAKER. 1921. Detroit kindergarten tests. Yonkers: World Book Company.

FULLERTON, G. S., and J. McK. CATTELL. 1892. On the perception of small differences. Philosophical Series of the Publications of the University of Pennsylvania, No. 2. Philadelphia: University of Pennsylvania Press. 159 pp.

FURFEY, P. H., and J. MUEHLENBEIN. 1932. The validity of infant intelligence tests. Journal of Genetic Psychology, 40:219-23.

GESELL, A. 1925. The mental growth of the preschool child. New York: Macmillan Company. x, 447 pp.

———— 1928. The mental growth of the preschool child: a psychological outline of normal development from birth to the sixth year, including a system of developmental diagnosis. New York: Macmillan Company. xvii, 418 pp.

GESELL, A., H. M. HALVERSON, et al. 1940. The first five years of life: the preschool years. New York: Harpers. xiii, 393 pp.

GODDARD, H. H. 1910. A measuring scale of intelligence. Vineland (New Jersey) Training School Bulletin No. 6, pp. 146–55.

———— 1911a. Two thousand normal children measured by the Binet measuring scale of intelligence. Pedagogical Seminary, 18:232–59.

———— 1911b. The Binet measuring scale for intelligence (revised edition). Vineland, New Jersey: The Training School. (Manual in record form.)

GOODENOUGH, F. L. 1926. The measurement of intelligence by drawings. Yonkers: World Book Company. xi, 177 pp.

———— 1928. The Kuhlmann-Binet tests for children of preschool age: a critical study and evaluation. Minneapolis. University of Minnesota Press. 146 pp.

———— 1929. The emotional behavior of young children during mental tests. Journal of Juvenile Research, 13:204–19.

———— 1931. Anger in young children. Minneapolis: University of Minnesota Press. xiii, 278 pp.

———— 1934. An early intelligence test. Child Development, 5:13–18.

GOODENOUGH, F. L., KATHARINE M. MAURER, and M. J. VAN WAGENEN. 1940. The Minnesota preschool scale (revised manual). Minneapolis: Educational Test Bureau.

HEIDBREDER, E. 1924. An experimental study of thinking. Archives of Psychology, No. 73. 175 pp.

HERRING, A. 1937. An experimental study of the reliability of the Bühler baby tests. Journal of Experimental Education, 6:147–60.

HERRING, J. P. 1922. The Herring revision of the Binet-Simon tests. Yonkers: World Book Company. 56 pp.

HILDRETH, G. H. 1926. Stanford-Binet retests of 441 school children. Pedagogical Seminary, 33:365–86.

———— 1939. A bibliography of mental tests and rating scales. Second edition. New York: Psychological Corporation. xxiv, 295 pp.

HILDRETH, G. H., and N. L. GRIFFITHS. 1933–39. Metropolitan readiness tests. Yonkers: World Book Company.

HONZIK, M. P. 1938. The constancy of mental test performance during the preschool period. Journal of Genetic Psychology, 52:285–302.

JAFFA, A. S. 1934. The California preschool mental scale. University of California Syllabus Series, No. 251. Berkeley: University of California Press. 66 pp.

KAWIN, E. 1934. Children of preschool age: studies in socio-economic status, social adjustment, and mental ability. Chicago: University of Chicago Press. xxv, 340 pp.

KELLEY, T. L. 1916. Simplified method of using scaled data for purposes of testing. School and Society, 4:34–37, 71–75.

KNOX, H. G. 1914. A scale based on the work at Ellis Island for estimating mental defects. Journal of the American Medical Association, 62:741–47.

KUHLMANN, F. 1922. A handbook of mental tests. Baltimore: Warwick and York. 208 pp.

———— 1939. Test of mental development: a complete scale for individual examination. Minneapolis: Educational Test Bureau. 314 pp.

LINFERT, H. E., and H. M. HIERHOLZER. 1928. A scale for measuring the mental development of infants during the first year of life. Studies in Psychology and Psychiatry, Catholic University of America, Vol. I, No. 4. 34 pp.

PINTNER, R., and B. CUNNINGHAM. 1923–29. Pintner-Cunningham Tests. Yonkers: World Book Company.

PINTNER, R., and D. G. PATERSON. 1917. A scale of performance tests. New York: D. Appleton and Company. xii, 218 pp.

PORTEUS, S. D. 1915. Mental tests for the feebleminded: a new series. Journal of Psycho-Asthenics, 19:200–13.

PREYER, W. 1882. Die Seele des Kindes. Leipzig: Fernau. (Fifth edition, 1900, 462 pp.) English edition, H. W. Brown, translator. 1888–89. The mind of the child.

Part I. The senses and the will. Part II. The development of the intellect. New York: D. Appleton and Company. 346, 317 pp.

REYNOLDS, M. M. 1928. Negativism of preschool children. Teachers College Contributions to Education, No. 288. New York: Columbia University. vi, 126 pp.

ROFF, M. F. 1941. A statistical study of the development of intelligence test performance. Journal of Psychology, 11:371–86.

ROSSILIMO, G. 1911. Die psychologische Profile. Zur Methodik der Quantitativen. Untersuchung der pathologischen Follen. Klinik für psychische und nervöse Krankheiten, Vol. 6, Nos. 3 and 4.

RUST, M. M. 1931. The effect of resistance on intelligence test scores. Child Development Monographs, No. 6. New York: Columbia University. xi, 80 pp.

SCUPIN, E., and G. SCUPIN. 1907. Bubi's erste Kindheit. Leipzig: Grieben. 264 pp.

SHEFFIELD, H. B. 1915. The backward baby. New York: Rebman Company.

SHINN, M. W. 1900. The biography of a baby. Boston: Houghton Mifflin Company. 247 pp.

SHIRLEY, M. 1931. The first two years: a study of twenty-five babies. Vol. I. Postural and locomotor development. Minneapolis: University of Minnesota Press. xvi, 227 pp.

——— 1933a. The first two years: a study of twenty-five babies. Vol. II. Intellectual development. Minneapolis: University of Minnesota Press. xv, 513 pp.

——— 1933b. The first two years: a study of twenty-five babies. Vol. III. Personality manifestations. Minneapolis: University of Minnesota Press. xi, 228 pp.

SHUTTLEWORTH, F. K. 1939. The physical and mental growth of girls and boys age six to nineteen in relation to age at maximum growth. Monographs of the Society for Research in Child Development, Vol. IV, No. 3. vi, 291 pp.

STERN, C., and W. STERN. 1909. Erinnerung, Aussage, und Luge in der ersten Kindheit. Monographien über die seelische Entwicklung des Kindes. Vol. II. Leipzig: Barth. x, 160 pp.

——— 1907. Die Kindersprache: eine psychologische und sprachtheoretische Untersuchung. Monographien über die seelische Entwicklung des Kindes. Vol. I. Leipzig: Barth. 394 pp. (Third edition revised, 1922, xii, 434 pp.)

STERN, W. 1914. Psychologie der frühen Kindheit, bis zum sechsten Lebensjahre. Leipzig: Quelle and Meyer. 372 pp. (Sixth edition revised, 1930, xiv, 539 pp.)

STUTSMAN, R. 1931. Mental measurement of preschool children. Yonkers: World Book Company. x, 368 pp.

TERMAN, L. 1916. The measurement of intelligence. Boston: Houghton Mifflin Company. xviii, 356 pp.

TERMAN, L., B. BURKS, and D. JENSEN. 1930. Genetic studies of genius. Vol. III. The promise of youth. Palo Alto, California: Stanford University Press. xiv, 508 pp.

TERMAN, L., and M. MERRILL. 1937. Measuring intelligence. Boston: Houghton Mifflin Company. xiv, 460 pp.

THORNDIKE, E. L. 1904. Introduction to the theory of mental and social measurements. New York: Science Press. xii, 212 pp.

TIEDEMANN, D. 1787. Beobachtungen über die Entwicklung der seelenfähigkeiten bei Kindern. (Edited by C. Ufer, Altenburg: Bonde Company, 1897.)

TRAXLER, A. 1941. IQ's obtained on the new edition of the Kuhlmann-Anderson tests and on the Binet scale. Elementary School Journal, 41:614–17.

VAN WAGENEN, M. J. 1925. Some implications of the revised Van Wagenen history scales. Teachers College Record, 27:142–48.

——— 1932. Van Wagenen reading readiness test. Minneapolis: Educational Test Bureau.

WELLMAN, B. L. 1938. The intelligence of preschool children as measured by the Merrill-Palmer scale of performance tests. University of Iowa Studies in Child Welfare, No. 15. 150 pp.

YERKES, R. M., and J. C. FOSTER. 1923. A point scale for measuring mental ability (revised). Baltimore: Warwick and York. viii, 219 pp.

AUTHOR INDEX

Anderson, J. E., 16, 21, 60, 113, 117, 118
Arthur, G., 11, 82, 89
Atkins, R. E., 10

Baker, H. J., 12
Bayley, N., 6, 13, 14, 15, 16, 55, 77, 98
Binet, A., 3, 29, 32
Bird, G., 12
Brown, R. W., 55
Bühler, C., 6
Burks, B., 98

Cattell, J. McK., 36, 37, 45
Cattell, P., 6
Chaille, S. E., 4
Conger, J., 14

Darley, J. G., 90, 95
Driscoll, G. P., 9

Ebert, E. H., 77, 78
Engel, A. M., 12

Foster, J. C., 8, 30
Fullerton, G. S., 36, 37
Furfey, P. H., 5, 13

Gesell, A., 5, 6, 27, 29, 32
Goddard, H. H., 3
Goodenough, F. L., 4, 8, 17, 20, 21, 23, 26, 32, 44, 47, 69, 78, 113
Griffiths, N. L., 12

Heidbreder, E., 62
Herring, A., 6
Hierholzer, H. M., 5
Hildreth, G. H., 11, 12, 55
Honzik, M. P., 15, 16, 55

Jaffa, A. S., 10
Jensen, D., 98

Kawin, E., 9
Kelley, T. L., 39, 76, 93
Knox, H. G., 28
Kuhlmann, F., 5, 17, 26, 28, 29, 31, 32

Linfert, H. E., 5

Merrill, M., 6, 8, 47, 78, 79
Muehlenbein, J., 13

Paterson, D. G., 28
Pintner, R., 28
Preyer, W., 4

Reynolds, M. M., 69
Roff, M. F., 64, 118
Rust, M. M., 69

Scupin, E., 4
Scupin, G., 4
Sheffield, H. B., 5
Shinn, M. W., 4
Shirley, M., 6, 13
Shuttleworth, F. K., 51
Stern, C., 4
Stern, W., 4
Stutsman, R., 8, 9, 11, 27, 30, 65, 66, 70

Terman, L., 6, 7, 8, 11, 28, 30, 31, 47, 76, 78, 79, 98
Thorndike, E. L., 35
Tiedemann, D., 4
Traxler, A., 78

Van Wagenen, M. J., 12, 35, 40

Wellman, B. L., 10
Woodrow, H., 11

Yerkes, R. M., 8, 30

SUBJECT INDEX